The Vestry Book — of — Henrico Parish Virginia 1730-1773

FROM THE ORIGINAL MANUSCRIPT

— WITH —

NOTES AND APPENDIX

Dr. Robert Alonzo Brock

HERITAGE BOOKS
2016

HERITAGE BOOKS
AN IMPRINT OF HERITAGE BOOKS, INC.

Books, CDs, and more—Worldwide

For our listing of thousands of titles see our website
at
www.HeritageBooks.com

A Facsimile Reprint
Published 2016 by
HERITAGE BOOKS, INC.
Publishing Division
5810 Ruatan Street
Berwyn Heights, Md. 20740

Originally published c. 1773

— Publisher's Notice —
In reprints such as this, it is often not possible to remove blemishes from the original. We feel the contents of this book warrant its reissue despite these blemishes and hope you will agree and read it with pleasure.

International Standard Book Numbers
Paperbound: 978-1-55613-506-4
Clothbound: 978-0-7884-6357-0

AT a VESTRY, held October the twenty Eight, in the Year of OUR LORD ONE THOUSAND SEVEN HUNDRED AND THIRTY, at CURLES[1] Church.

Prefent.

The Reverend Mr. James Keith,

Richard Randolph,[2]	John Worfham,
John Redford,	Jofeph Royal,
Bowler Cocke,	John Bolling.

Henrico Parifh. *Dr.*

To the Reverend James Keith,	*	
To William Perkins, Reader,		
To Richard Williams, ditto,		
To Charles Griffith, ditto,		
To Do. Clerk of the Veftry,		
To John Hobfon, Sexton,		
To John Ofborn, Ditto,		
To Thomas Branch, for Ferriages,		
To Thomas Jefferfon,[3] Do.		
To Joseph Wilkinfon, for Ann Hewett,		
To the Church-wardens for the poor, viz :		
Abraham Robinfon,		
Pardue's Sons,		
To Jofeph Wilkinson,		
To Sarah Woodcock, for her fon,		
To Hutchins Burton, for Sarah Rawlins,		
To John Herbert,		
To Abraham Bailey, for John Worth,		
Brought over,	† 25,800	1,164
To Elizabeth Womack, for keeping a foundling child fix months,	500	40
To the Church-wardens, for Sufanna Wakefield,	800	64
To Richard Williams, Sexton,	600	

*Figure illegible in original.

†Pounds of Tobacco.

To Capt[e] John Redford, for the railing of the Church, in full payment,	4,000	320
To William Bafs, ditto,	4,000	200
To Capt[e] John Redford, for fix Benches,	200	16
To William Robertfon, for keeping Andrew Crawford four months and burying of him,	1,000	80
To Capt[e] Jofeph Royal, for twenty-nine levies, entered in the lift and live in King William parifh,	1,131	
To Ditto, for nine Infolvents,	351	
To Col[o] Francis Epps, as Per Acct.,	1,113	
To Jofeph Royal, for five Tithables, twice lifted,	195	
To Jofeph Royal, Collect'd for good paiment,	541	
	40,231	2,904
Sallary,	4,023	
Cafk,[4]	2,904	
	47,158	
Due to the Parifh,	62	
	47,220	

Henrico Parifh *Cr.*

By 1574 Tithables at 30lb of Tob'o Per pole, 47,220

Ordered,

That Capt[e] Jofeph Royal to receive, according to law, of Every Tithable p'fon within this parifh, thirty pounds of tobacco, being the parifh levy for this year, and that he pay the Several Allowances before mentioned to the refpective perfons to whom the fame are due.

JAMES KEITH, Minifter.

AT A VESTRY held for HENRICO PARISH, the Twenty-Seventh of September, in the Year of Our Lord One Thoufand Seven Hundred and thirty One.

Prefent.

Jofeph Royal, church-warden; Francis Eppes, John Redford, Bowler Cocke, Edward Booker, James Powel Cocke and John Worfham, Jofeph Mayo[5] and William Worfham, Gentlemen take the Oath of Veftrymen for the Parifh.

Prefent, Jofeph and William Worfham, Gent.

Purfuant to an Act of Affembly of this Colony, directing due manner of proceffioning of lands, &c.,[6] the ffollowing precincts are lay'd out and directed to be proceffioned for the parifh aforefaid, vizt: the North fide lower precinct from Turkey Ifland Creek up to four Mile Creek, between White Oak Swamp and the River, and that part of this parifh from the lower line between White Oak and Chiquohomony as high as Thomas Matthew's plantation.

Prefent, the Reverend James Keith.

Jofeph Pleafants and Stephen Woodfon are appoint'd to fee the proceffioning made to the lower precinct, on the North fide between the River and Swamp, and John Cocke and Thomas Wilkins in the precinct, back between the two Swamps and four mile creek.

From ffour Mile Creek to the River at the Mouth of ffield's Creek, all Within the Main Road to the River, John Redford and Benjamin Burton are appointed to see proceffioned.

From ffour Mile Creek bridge above the Said Creek, croffing Northerly as the Said Creek tendeth to the head, and thence Out to Thomas Matthew's, thence up Chiquohomony Swamp to upland Brook bridge, thence as the road tendeth to Rocketts, thence to the Mouth of ffield's Creek, thence to the place began at, by Joell Walker and James Cocke to be proceffioned.

From upland brook bridge, up the branch to the head to John Walford's on Do., thence down the faid Run to Tuckahoe Creek, thence as the faid Creek tendeth to the River, thence down the River to Rocketts, to be proceffioned by John Price and John Williamfon.

From the Mouth of Deeprun up Tuckahoe to the Mouth of Chumbley's branch, thence along the County line to Hanover line, thence down Chiquohomony Swamp to the Mouth of upland Brook, thence up the Brook to the bridge, to be proceffioned by Robert Mofby and John Shepherd.

The ffirst precinct on the South fide James River, to begin at the mouth of powel's Creek, Running up the river to the Ware run, thence up the faid Run to the Appomattox Road, thence along the faid Road to the parifh line, thence down the faid Line to the place began at, to be proceffioned by William Mofeley and Robert Ealam.

From the Mouth of Ware run up the river to the Mouth of ffalling Creek, thence up the Said Creek Oppofite to Tallies' Old plantation, thence acrofs to Grill's Old plantation on Swift Creek, thence down the faid Creek to the parifh Line, thence along the Said Line to Appomattox Road, thence along the faid Road to the place began at, to be proceffioned by Henry Vanderhood and ffield Jefferfon.[7]

From the Mouth of ffalling Creek up the river to the Mouth of Powhite Creek, thence up the Said Creek to Lucy's Spring, thence croffing to Lodwick Tanner's on Swift Creek, thence down the faid Creek to Grill's Plantation, thence acrofh to Tullitt's Old plantation, thence down ffalling Creek to the Mouth thereof, to be proceffioned by Wharham Eafly and Thomas Harris.

ffrom the Mouth of Powhite up the River to the parifh line, thence along the parifh Lines to the County Lines, thence along the County line to Swift Creek, thence down the Creek to Lodowicks Tanner's, thence to the Mouth of Powhite Creek to be proceffioned by John James Fflourenoy and Francis fflournoy.

From parifh line on the South fide Swift Creek, along the faid Line to Appomattox River, thence up the faid River to the Mouth of Middle Creek, thence to Swift Creek, as Straight a Courfe as may be gueffed, to Robert Arfhurst's plantations, thence down the faid Creek to the place began at, to be proceffioned by William Locket and Benjamin Loket, Jun'r.

From the Mouth of Middle Creek on Appomattox River, up the Same to the County Line, thence along the said Line to

Swift Creek, thence down the faid Creek to the faid Robert Arfhurft's plantation, thence to the head of Middle Creek, thence down the faid Creek to the place began at, to be proceffioned by Edward Hafkins and Creed Haskins.

JAMES KEITH.

At a Vestry held for the parifh of Henrico, at CURLES Church, October the Eleventh, in the Year of Our Lord One Thoufand Seven Hundred and Thirty-one.

Prefent.

The Reverend Mr. James Keith.

William Randolph, Efq[8]	Richard Randolph,
Francis Eppes,	John Redford,
James Powel Cocke,	Bowler Cocke,
Edward Booker,	William Worfham,
Jofeph Mayo,	John Worfham.

Henrico Parifh.	*Dr.*	
To the Reverend James Keith,	16,000	64
To William Perkins, Reader,	2,000	80
To Richard Williams, Reader,	1,680	69
To Charles Griffith, Reader,	2,000	80
To Do. Clerk of the Veftry,	500	80
To John Hobfon, Sexton,	600	25
To John Ofborn, Do	600	28
To Thomas Branch, fferriages,	1,200	48
To Peter Jefferfon, Son and Ex'r. of Thomas Jefferfon, and to ffield Jefferfon, Brother to the faid Peter Jefferfon, for fferriages,	1,200	48
To Jofeph Wilkinson, for Ann Hewett,	1,200	48
To the Church wardens for the floor, viz:		
To Abraham Robinfon,	1,400	
To Jofeph Williamfon,	800	
To Elianos Clerk, for keeping John Spring five weeks,	300	
To Sufanna Woodcocke, for her fon,	200	
To Hutchins Burton, for Sarah Rawlins,	700	28
To John Herbert,	1,000	40

To Capt[e] Jofeph Royal, for Sufanna Wakefield,	800	32
To Elianor Williams, as Sexton, for her Own Ufe	600	24
To the Church wardens for Bread and Wine laft year,	400	
To Michael Taylor, for John Littleworth,	400	
To Abraham Bayley, for keeping John Littleworth two months,	133	
To the Church-wardens for bread and Wine this Year,	100	
To Sufanna Ware, for curing John Weft's hand,	800	
To Mary Harding, for curing Mary Burnet of a Burn,	240	
To Mary Harding, for keeping Mary Burnet three Months,	300	
To John Synock, for putting up the Glafs of the Church Winder,	10	
To the Reverend James Keith, 14 per ct. on his Sallary,	2,616	
To the Church-warden, toward repairing the Chapple,	1,000	
	38,779	1,343

Ordered,

That William Randolph, Efq, and Mr. Edward Booker, be appointed Church-wardens.

Ordered,

That Elianor Williams be continued as Sexton of the Chapple

Ordered,

Sackfield Brewer be appointed Reader in the Chapple, Richard Williams being abfconded from his duty therein.

Ordered,

That the Veftry do meet at the Court Houfe, on Saturday next, to proportion the Parifh Levy, this Veftry not to be able to do the fame, by reafon, the lift of Tithables is not Complete.

JAMES KEITH.

AT A VESTRY, held for the Parifh of HENRICO, in the county of Henrico, November the Second, in the Year of Our Lord One Thousand Seven Hundred and thirty-one.

Prefent.

The Reverend James Keith.

Francis Epps,		Richard Randolph,
Bowler Cocke,		Jofeph Mayo,
John Bolling,[6]		John Worfham,
Edward Booker,	and	James Powel Cocke.

Henrico Parifh,	*Dr.*	
To Brought forward,	38,779	1,343
To Capt[e] Jofeph Royal, for Eight Infolvents, at 39 lbs. Tob'o,	272	
To Seth Ward, for Infolvents,	420	
To Capt[e] Jofeph Royal, as per aacc't,	512	
To Edward Bennett, for a Levy over charged in the year 1729,	39	
	40,022	
Sallary at 4 lbs. Per Ct.,	1,601	
Cafk,	1,343	
	43,012	
Balance due to the Parish,	46	
	43,012	

Henrico Parish,	*Cr.*
By Josefh Royal, for a ballance due in the Year 1729,	110
By " for " due in the Year 1730,	62
By 1680 Tithables at 25½ lbs Tb'o per poll,	42,840
	43,012

Ordered,

That Capt^e Henry Anderfon do receive, According to Law, of Every Tithable perfon Within the parifh, twenty-five pounds and a half of tobacco being the parifh Levy for this year, and that he pay the Several Allowances before mentioned to the refpective persons to whom the fame are due.

JAMES KEITH.

At a Vestry held for the parifh of HENRICO, at Curles Church the thirteenth day of October, in the Year of Our Lord One Thoufand and Seven Hundred and thirty-two.

Prefent.

The Reverend Mr. James Keith.

William Randolph,	Francis Eppes,
Richard Randolph,	Joseph Royal,
Bowler Cocke,	Edward Booker,
James Powel Cocke,	John Worfham,
William Worfham,	John Bolling.

Henrico Parish.	*Dr.*	
To the Reverend Mr. James Keith,	16,000	640
To William Perkins, Reader,	2,000	80
To Sackfield Brewer, Do.	2,000	80
To Charles Griffith, Do.	2,000	80
To Ditto, Clerk of the Vestry,	500	20
To John Hobfon, Sexton,	600	24
To Thomas Branch, for fferriage,	1,200	48
To ffield Jefferfon, for Do.	120	48
To Jofeph Wilkinson for keeping Ann Hewitt seven months,	700	28
To the Church Wardens for the Poor, viz:		
To Abraham Robinfon,	1,400	50
To Richard Wood for keeping Jofeph Williamfon,	800	32
To Elianor Williams, Sexton of the Chapple,	600	24
To Sufanna Wood for keeping her son,	1,200	48
To Hutchkins Burton for keeping Sarah Rawlins,	700	28

To Church wardens for bread and Wine,	400	
To 14 lb. per ct. on Mr. Keith's Sallary,	2,616	
To Capt. Jofeph Royal under cafk in Eight Infolvents laft year,	40	
To William Pardue,	600	24
To Elizabeth Bargeff for keeping Ann Bryant's child one year, ending the 18th December next,	800	
To Thomas Ofborne, Jun'r, for keeping a Baftard Child a year, ending the firft day of ffebruary next,	800	
To James Franklin for keeping Alice Bryant,	484	
To Philip Smith for keeping a Baftard Child fix months, ending the twenty-third day of Octob'r,	400	
To Ralph Jackfon for keeping two of Robert Blakeley's children,	250	
To Jofeph Watfon for keeping a bastard child three months,		
To Michael Taylor for keeping John Worth a year,	700	28
To Conveniency for Do. at 14 per cent.	98	
To William Ligon for keeping Mary Dundan,	600	24
To Conveniency for Do. at 14 per ct.,	84	
To Hays Whitloe for keeping William Weather one year,	700	
To Conveniency for Do. at 14 per ct.,	98	
To the Church warden for the ufe of John Tanner,	500	
To Jofeph Wilkinfon for burying Ann Hewet, and other charges in her sicknefs,	310	
To Elianor Clark for cureing and keeping Sufanna Wakefield two months,	800	
To Jofeph Royal for keeping Sufanna Wakefield,	500	
To John Nafh for Infolvents, and twice lifted perfons, and an Error in Cafting up one thoufand pounds of tobacco in laft levy,	1,419	

To William Randolph, Efq., towards two Surplus' and two Common Prayer Books,	2,500	
To William Cocke for 14 Infolvents, and perfons twice lifted,	406 281	
To John Smyth, a Grandfon of Humphrey Smyth, to be paid to the Church wardens,	300	
To Capt. Jofeph Royal for John Higdin's parifh levy,	30	
To Capt. Jofeph Royal for Conveniency on his Acc't laft year,	71	
To John Smart for a levy laft year,	25½	
	47,437½	1364
Sallary at 4 per cent.,	1,897½	
Cafk,	1,364	
	50,699	
Balance due to the Parifh,	213	
	50,912	

Henrico Parifh,	*Cr.*
By 1,754 Tithables, at 29 ℔ of Tob'o per poll,	50,866
By the laft year ballance due from the Collector,	46
	50,912

Richard Wood applying to this Veftry for a Maintainance of Jofeph Williamfon, an Idiot, and the Veftry being informed that he hath a Right to a Tract of land, containing about three hundred acres, which is unpatented, they are of Opinion the Value of faid Tract of Land Ought to be Apply'd for the Maintenance of the faid Jofeph Williamfon.

Whereupon the faid Richard agrees to keep the faid Jofeph for four years in Confideration that the Land may be granted to William* Law to the faid Jofeph, which this Veftry think reafonable, and humbly reprefent it to the Governor and Council for the Grant Accordingly.

*Illegible.

Ordered that Capt. Henry Anderfon do receive according to Law of Every tithable perfon within this parifh twenty-Nine pounds of Tobacco, being the parifh levy for this year—and that he pay the feveral allowances above Mentioned to the refpective perfons to whom the fame are due, for which Maj'r Richard Randolph and Capt. James Powel Cocke become Securitys.

Ordered,

That Capt. John Worfham be appointed Church-warden in the room of Mr. Edward Booker.

JAMES KEITH.

AT A VESTRY held the Second day of March, in the Year of Our Lord One thoufand Seven hundred and thirty-two.

Prefent.

The Reverend Mr. James Keith.

William Randolph,	Richard Randolph,
Jofeph Royal,	Bowler Cocke,
James Powel Cocke,	John Worfham,

and William Worfham.

Charles Griffith, Reader of the lower Church in this parifh being dead, Stephen Dewey is appointed to succeed him.

Ordered,

That Stephen Dewey be appointed Clerk of the Veftry, in the Room of Charles Griffith, deceafed.

Mr. Edward Booker, one of the Veftry of this Parifh being removed, Mr. Arthur Mofeley is appointed to succeed him.

JAMES KEITH, *Minifter.*

AT A VESTRY held for Henrico parifh, the twelfth day of Oct'r., in the Year of Our Lord One Thousand Seven hundred and thirty-three.

Prefent.

William Randolph, Efq'r,	Francis Eppes,
Bowler Cocke,	James Powel Cocke,
John Worfham,	William Worfham.

And Mr. Arthur Mofeley being at the laft Veftry elected a Veftryman for Henrico parifh, now takes an Oath to Execute that Office truly and to be Conformable to the Doctrines and Difcipline of the Church of England.

Ordered,

That the Veftry proceed to the laying of the Parifh levy.

Henrico Parifh,	*Dr.*	
To the Reverend Mr. James Keith, Minister,	16,000	640
To William Perkins, one of the Readers,	2,000	80
To ffield Brown Do.	2,000	80
Eales Do. a Year ending the Second of March next,	2,000	80
To Stephen Dewey, Clerk of the Veftry, a Year ending the Second of March next,	500	20
To John Hobfon, Sexton,	600	24
To John Ofborn Do.	600	24
To Thomas Branch for fferriage,	1,200	48
To ffield Jefferfon for Do.	1,200	48
To the Church-wardens for the poor,		
To Abraham Robinfon,	1,400	56
Woodcocke for keeping her fon,	1,200	48
To Hutchkins Burton, for keeping Sufanna Rawlins,	700	28
To Jofeph Ligon for keeping Littleworth three months and a half, and burying him,	536	22
To for the time he kept him,	100	
To Hutchkins Burton for keeping Sufanna Rollins,	700	28
To Mary North for keeping Sufanna Burnett,	1,000	40
To Robert Bullington for keeping William Watkins,	800	28
To 14 per ct. for Convenience on Do.	112	
To Thomas Gibfon for keeping William Hobfon by 5½ Months,	350	28
To James Aiken, Jun'r., for keeping faid Hobby by five weeks,	125	

To Abel Turner for keeping James Wood four Months, Ending Nov'r Twelft next,	266	10
To Richard Randolph, Gent. for and Ells oz-nabs. for Wm. Hobby,	60	
To 4 per ct. for Conveniency,	8	
To William Pride for keeping Jas. Wood 2 Months, and for Some Cloaths for the faid Wood,	282	11
To the Church-wardens for Bread and Wine,	400	
To 14 per ct. on Mr. Keith's Sallary for Conveniency,	2,616	
To Sarah Herbert for burying John Frayfer,	200	
To John Bolling, Gent. for keeping and Burying John Hance,	200	
To Ezekiel Sudbury for Burying Henry Exon,	200	
To Seth Ward for Burying John Warwick,	80	
Due to the Collectors for Infolvens and perfons twice lifted,	250	
To ffield Jefferfon for Siting up horfe blocks at the Church,	100	
	36,615	129
Sallary at 4 per ct.	1,517	
Cafk,	1,290	
	39,422	129
	39,226	
	196	
	39,442	

Ordered,

That John Nafh and William Fuller do receive according to Law of every Tithable perfon within this parifh Twenty-two pounds of Tobacco, being the parifh levy for this year, and that they pay the feveral allowances before mentioned to the refpective persons to whom Same are Due. Bowler Cocke and Jas. Powel Cocke Gent. Securities.

Ordered,

That the refignation of Mr. James Keith[10] as Minister of this Parifh be received.

Ordered,

That the Church Wardens of this parifh in behalf of the Veftry do make a reprefentation hereof to the Governor.

WILLIAM RANDOLPH, *Ch. War'n.*

AT A VESTRY held at Curl's Church, for Henrico Parifh, ye 17th day of June, 1735.

Prefent.

William Randolph, Efq'r, Richard Randolph, Bowler Cocke and James Powell Cocke, Gent. Vefftrymen.

Purfuant to the directions of an Act of Assembly, directing the Dividing of Henrico parifh, the freeholders and houfekeepers preffent do unanimously Ellect Edward Curd, John Williamfon, James Cocke, John Povall and Robt. Mofsby, which with ye Veftrymen, formerly of this parifh, make up the number twelve, who take the Oaths and Subfcribe ye Declarations as Veftrymen.

I do Sincerely promife and Swear to be Conformable to the Doctrine and Difcipline of the Church of England, June ye 17th, 1735.

EDWARD CURD,
JOHN WILLIAMSON,
JAMES COCKE,
JOHN POVALL,
ROBERT MOSBY,
WILLIAM FULLER

Order.

James powel Cocke and James Cocke Gent. are Ellected Church Wardens for this parifh.

The Veftry agree that Mr. Zach. Brook do preach a day in every fifth week at the falls Chappel, and Mr. David Moffon[11] every fifth Sunday at the Church, for which they are to be Allowed four hundred pounds of Tob'o p. Sermon.

Sackville Brewer is continued Reader of this Church and Clerk of ye Veftry.

John Eals is continued Reader of ye Chappel.
John Hobfon is continued Sexton of this Church.
Elenor Williams is continued Sexton at ye Chappel.

AT A VESTRY held at Curl's Church Sunday Morning September ye 2nd, 1735.

Prefent.

James Powel Cocke, James Cocke, Richard Randolph, John Redford, Bowler Cocke, John Bolling, Edward Curd, John Povall, John Williamfon and Robt. Mofby Gent., Veftrymen.

The Rev'd Mr. Anthony Gavin produces a letter from the Hon'ble William Gooch, Effqr., his Maj's Lieut. Governor of this Colony, and another from the Rev'd James Blair, Commiffary, directed to the Church Wardens and Gent. of the Veftry, recommending the faid Mr. Gavin to the care of this Parifh, which are Read, and the Veftry being defirous of firftt hearing him performe the Office of his Minifterial function, do fufpend their Opinion as to his reception till after Sermon, when they do agree to meet again.

Whereas, the Rev'd Anthony Gavin hath performed his office both in reading and preaching to the General Satiffaction and appreciation of the Veftry, it is thereupon unanimoufly agreed that he be received and entertained as Minifter of this Parifh. And it is thereupon Ordered that the Church Wardens do Answer the Governor's and Commiffary's letters, and inform them of the proceedings herein.

JAMES POWEL COCKE,
Church Warden.

AT A VESTRY held at Curl's Church, for Henrico parifh, for laying the parifh levy, November the 24th, 1735.

Prefent.

The Rev'd Anthony Gavin, Min'r, James Powel Cocke and James Cock, Church-wardens, William Randolph, Effqr., Richard Randolph, John Redford, Bowler Cocke, John Bolling, Edward Curd, and John Williamson Gent. Veftrymen.

Henrico Parifh, *Dr.*

	Tobacco.	Cafk.
To Ballance due to the Collector laft year,	196	
To Mr. Moffon for preaching four Sermons, at 500 per,	2,000	
To Do. for three Sermons, at 400,	1,200	
To 14 per ct. on said 1,200 for Conveniency,	168	
To John Ealls, Reader at Chappell,	2,000	80
To Sackvil Brewer, Reader,	2,000	80
To Do. as Clerk of the Veftry,	500	20
To John Hobfon, Sexton,	600	24
To Elenor Williams Do. at Chappell,	600	24
To the Church-wardens for Bread and Wine,	400	
To Sufanna Woodcock for keeping her Son,	1,200	48
To Collector on Northfide for Infolvents Acc't,	418	
To Do. for Northfide of James River for Do.	264	
To William perkins, Reader for Seven Months,	1,167	46
To John Ofborn, Sexton for Seven Months,	350	14
To Mr. Brook for preaching at the Chappel,	1,600	
To Thomas Branch yr. proportion of Seven Months ferriage,	381	14
To Walter Scot for keeping John Lyle,	400	
To Robert Bullington for keeping and burying Wm. Withers,	1,200	
To William Randolph, Effqr., for Beding for said Withers,	168	
To 14 per cent. on Do. for Conveniency,	1,680	
To ye Clerk of the Court for Copping Two Laws,	80	
To Elenor Turner for keeping James Wood,	150	
To Ralph Jackfon for keeping Wm. Hobby,	350	
To Hutchkins Burton for keeping Sufanna Rollins,	700	28
To Mary North for keeping Sufanna Burnet,	1,000	40
To Mr. Anthony Gavin, pt. of his firft year's Sallary,	12,000	480
To 14 per cent. on Do. for Conveniency,	1,680	

To Lemmon Childers for burying Weft, and taking care of his Child,	600	
To Elizabeth Burges for keeping John Lyle two years,	1,600	
	35,376	912
Cafk,	912	
	36,288	
Commiffion at 4 per cent,	1,452	
	37,740	

Henrico Parifh,	*Cr.*
By Tobacco Levy'd in Dale parifh Neck,	4,136
By 1,013 Tithables, at 33 pounds Tobacco per pole,	33,429
Ballance due to the Collector,	175
	37,740

It is ordered that John Nafh, Gent, do receive of every Tithable perfon of this parifh Thirty-three pounds of Tobacco, being the parifh Levey for this year; and if any perfon refufes to pay the same he is to Difftrain for it, and pay unto each parifh creditor reffpectively their feveral sums of Tobacco as in the proportions of the faid Levy are mentioned, for the performance of which the faid John Nafh Enters into Bond, Bowler Cocke and John Bolling, Gent. Securitys.

Mr. William Fuller is Choffen a Veftryman in the Room of Jofeph Mayo, Gent. who is willing to reffign the place the said ffuller take the Oaths as A Veftryman, and Signs the Declaration accordingly.

prefent William Fuller.

on the Motion of mr. Anthony Gavin, the Veftry do agree to make all neceffary Reparations to the Gleeb House, and to build a Kitchen Twenty-four feet long and Sixteen feet broad, to be under-pined with Brick, and an infide Brick Chimney.

Richard Randolph and Edward Curd, Gent. are appointed

to view the Chappel and report what reparation and Additions are thereunto wanting.

It is ordered that Mr. John Nafh, Collector of this parifh do receive of every Tithable in the faid parifh Six pence Curr't. money, or five pounds of Tobacco, to be employ'd towards repairing the Chappel.

Ant. Gavin, Min'r., Jas. powel Cocke, James Cocke, Church Wardens.

AT A VESTRY held at Curl's Church, for Henrico parifh, the Sixth day of December, Ano. 1735.

Prefent.

James powel Cocke, James Cocke, Church Wardens; William Randolph, Effqr., Richard Randolph, Bowler Cocke, John Redford, John povall, John Williamfon, Robert Mofby and William Fuller, Gent., Veftrymen.

Purfuant to an Act of Affembly of this Colony, directing the manner of proceffioning every perfon's Land, and the following precinct are laid out and Directed to be proceffioned as follows, Viz.:

In Obedience to an Act of Affembly of this Colony, and in purfuance of an order of Henrico County Court, made at a Court held for the faid County the firft day of December, anno 1735: The Veftry do order that John Ellis, William Ellis and Abraham Childers, with the Affiftance of the Neighboring freeholders, do fome time before the laft day of March Next coming, goe in proceffion and renew the bounds of all the Land adjoining on James River, between Weftham and the upper bounds of the parifh, to Extend back as far as Gordin's Road, that leads up to Rocketts; and that the faid John Ellis, William Ellis and Abraham Childers, (or any two of them,) do take and return to this parifh Veftry an Account of every perfon's Land they fhall proceffion, and of ye perfons prefent at the fame, and of what Lands in their precinct they fhall fail to proceffion, and of the particular reafon of fuch failure.

Purfuant to an Act of Affembly of this Colony, and in Obedience to an Order of Henrico County Court, made at a Court held for the faid County the firft day of December, ano. 1735. The Veftry do order that Jofeph parfons, Thomas

Owen, and William Brittain, with the Affiftance of ye Neighboring freeholders, do Sometime before the laftt day of March Next coming, go in proceffion and renew the bounds of all the Land from William Gordin's on the back Road to the head of ye parifh, thence to the Main Swamp so Down to Turner's Run, thence up Hungary Branch to the head of upland Brook, thence to Gordin's aforefaid; and that the faid Jofeph parfon, Thomas owin and William Britain, (or any two of them,) do take and return to this parifh Veftry an account of every perfon's land they fhall proceffion, and of the perfons prefent at the Same, and all lands in their precinct they fhall fail to proceffion, and of the particular reafon of fuch failure.

Purfuant to an Act of Affembly of this Colony, and in Obedience to an order of Henrico County Court, made at a Court held for the faid County the firft day of December, ano. 1735; The Veftry do order that John Watfon, John Williamfon and Wm. patman, with the Affiftance of the Neighboring freeholders, do Sometime before the laft day of March Next coming, goe in proceffion and renew the bounds of all the lands between upland Brook and Chickahominy Swamp, and that the faid John Watfon, John Williamfon and William patman, (or any two of them,) do take and return to this parifh Veftry an Account of every perfon's land they shall proceffion, and of the perfons prefent at the Same, and of what Land in their precinct they fhall Fail to proceffion, and of the particular Reafon of Such Failure.

Purfuant to an Act of Affembly of this Colony in Obedience to an Order of Henrico County Court, made at a Court held for the Said County the firft day of December, ano. 1735: The Veftry do order that Joel Walker, Henry Stokes and John Smith, with the Affiftance of the Neighboring freeholders, do Sometime before the laft day of March Next coming, goe in proceffion and renew the bounds of all lands between Chickahominy Swamp and the Brook Road, as low as Mary Cannon's and Smith's Mill; and that the faid Joel Walker, Henry Stokes and John Smith, (or any two of them,) do take and return to this parifh Veftry and Account of every perfon's land they shall proceffion, and of the perfons prefent at the fame, and of what land in their precincts they fhall fail to proceffion, and the particular reafon of fuch failure.

Purfuant to an Act of Affembly of this Colony, and in Obedience to an order of Henrico County Court, made at a Court held for the faid County the firft day of December, ano. 1735: The Veftry do order that Thomas Wood, Hutchkins burton and John price, with the Affiftance of the Neighboring freeholders do Sometime before the laft day of March Next coming, go in proceffion and Renew the bounds of all lands adjoining on the River between Gilly's Creek and Weftham, to Extend back as far as Mary Cannon's and William Gordin's, and that the faid Thomas Wood, Hutchkins Burton and John price, (or any two of them,) do take and return to this parifh Veftry an Account of every perfon's land they fhall proceffion, and of the perfons prefent at ye Same, and of what land in their precincts they fhall fail to proceffion, and the particular reafon of Such failure.

Purfuant to an Act of Affembly of this Colony, and in Obedience to an Order of Henrico County Court, at a Court held for the faid County, the firft day of December, ano. 1735: The Veftry do order that William Lewis, Henry Hatcher and Daniel price, with the Affiftance of the Neighboring freeholders, do Sometime before the laft day of March Next coming, go in proceffion and renew the bounds of all lands from the Mouth of Gilley's Creek to William Lewis's, on Chickahominy Swamp, thence up the faid Swamp to Smith's mill, thence to Mary Cannon's, to the place firft Mentioned, and that ye faid Wm. Lewis, Henry Hatcher and Daniel price, (or any two of them,) do take and return to this parifh Veftry an Account of every perfon's Land they fhall proceffion, and the perfons prefent at the Same, and of what land in their precinct they fhall fail to proceffion, and the particular reafon of fuch failure.

Purfuant to an Act of Affembly of this Colony, and in obedience to an order of Henrico County Court, held for the said County, the firft day of December, ano. 1735: The Veftry do order that John Giles, Thomas Mofby and John Allday, with the Affiftance of the Neighboring freeholders, do Sometime before the laft day of March Next coming, goe in proceffion, and renew the bounds of all Lands adjoining on the River between Gilly's Creek and Cornealiouf's, Extending back as far as ye Seven pines Road, as low as the Southern

Branch Bridge, and that the faid John Giles, John Aulday and Thomas Mofby, (or any two of them,) do take and return to this parifh Veftry, an account of every perfon's Land they fhall proceffion, and ye perfons prefent at the Same, and of what Land in their precinct they fhall fail to proceffion, and the particular reafons of fuch failure.

Purfuant to an Act of Affembly of this Colony, and in Obedience to an order of Henrico County Court, Made at a Court for the Said County, the firft day of December, ano. 1735: The Veftry do order that John Stuart, Ewd. Cox and Benjamin Burton, with ye Affiftance of the Neighboring free holders, do Sometime before the laft day of March Next coming, goe in proceffion and renew the bounds of all lands included, Corneliuf's, Twomile Creek, ye Main Roade, And that the Said John Stuart, Edward Cox and Benjamin Burton, or any two of them, do take and return to this parifh Veftry an Account of every perfons Land they fhall proceffion, and the perfons prefent at the Same, and of what Land they fhall fail to proceffion, and the particular Reafon of Such failure.

Purfuant to an Act of Affembly of this Colony, and in obedience to an order of Henrico County Court, at a Court held for the faid County, the firft day of December, ano. 1735: The Veftry order that John Redford, junr., Abraham Childers and Henry Sharp, with the Affiftance of the Neighboring free holders, do Sometime before the laft of March Next coming, go in proceffion and renew the bounds of all the Lands between Two Mile Creek, four mile Creek and the main Road, and that the Said John Redford, Henry Sharp and Abraham Childers, (or any two of them,) do take and return to this parifh Veftry an Account of every perfon's Land they fhall proceffion, and the perfons prefent, and of what land in their precincts they fhall fail to proceffion, and the pareicular reafon of fuch failure.

Purfuant to an Act of Affembly of this Colony, and in Obedience to an order of Henrico County Court, and at a Court held for ye Said County, the firft day of December, ano. 1735: The Veftry do order that Jofeph Adkins, William Whitloe and Darby Enroughty, with the Affiftance of the Neighboring freeholders, Sometime before the laft day of March Next Coming, go in proceffion and renew the bounds of all Lands between Corneliuf's and four Mile Creek, from ye Main Road back as far as the Seven pines Road, and that the Said Jofeph Adkins, William Whitloe, and Darby Enroughty,[12] (or any two of them,) do take and return to this parifh Veftry an account of all lands by them proceffioned, and the perfon prefent at the fame, and of What Land they fhall fail to proceffion in their precinct, and the particular reafon of fuch failure.

Purfuant to an Act of Affembly of this Colony, in Obedience to an order of Henrico County Court, made at a Court held for the Said County, the firft day of December, ano. 1735: The Veftry do order that Edward Allen, John Ferris and Richard Williamfon, with the Affiftance of ye Neighboring free holders, do Sometime before the laft day of the March Next Coming, goe in proceffion and Renew the bounds of all lands between William Lewif's, Bore's Swamp, the Main Swamp, and the Seven pines Road, and the Edward Allen, John Ferris and Richard Williamfon, or any two of the them, do take and return to the Veftry of this parifh an account of every perfon's Land they fhall proceffion, and the perfons prefent at the Same, and of all land they fhall fail to proceffion in their precinct, and the particular reafon of fuch failure.

Purfuant to an Act of Affembly of this Colony, and in obedience to the order of Henrico County Court, made at a Court held for ye faid County, this firft day of December, Ano. 1735: The Veftry do order that John Cocke, Gerrard Ellifon and Giles Carter, with the Affiftance of the Neighboring free holders, do Sometime before the laft day of March Next coming, goe in proceffion and renew the lands of all Lands from Bore Swamp, on Chickahominy Swamp, to the lower bounds of ye parifh, thence Southerly to the place where the long bridge road parts with Bottom Bridge Road, and that the faid John Cocke, Gerrard Ellifon and Giles Cocke, (or any two of them,) do take and return to their parifh Veftry an account of every perfon's Lands by them proceffioned, and the perfons prefent at the Same, and of all Land in their precinct they Shall fail to proceffion, and the particular reafons of Such failure.

Purfuant to an Act of Affembly of this Colony, and in Obedience to an order of Henrico County Court, Made at a

Court for the Said County, the firft day of December, Ano. 1735: The Veftry do order that Edward Goode, John Hobfon and Samuel Gathright, with the Affiftance of the Neighboring free holders, do Sometime before the laft day of March Next Coming, goe in proceffion and renew ye bounds of all land Between Baily's run and four mile Creek, as far as the Road that leads from Chickahominy Swamp to Varina, and that the said Edward Goode, John Hobfon and Samuel Gathright, or any two of them, do take & return to this parifh Veftry an Account of all the Lands they Shall proceffion, and the perfons prefent at the Same, and of all land in their precinct they fhall fail to proceffion, and the particular reafons of Such failure.

Purfuant to an Act of Affembly of this Colony, and in Obedience to an Order of Henrico County Court, Made at a Court held for ye County aforefaid, the firft day of December, Ano. 1735: The Veftry do order that Thomas pleafant, Steven Woodfon and Charles ffloyd, with the Affiftance of the Neighboring free holders, do Sometime before the laft day of March Next coming, go in proceffion and renew the bounds of all lands between Baily's Run and the lower bound of the parifh, to Extend back as far as Weftern Run, and the faid Tho. pleafants, Steven Woodfon and Charles floyd, or any two of them, do take and return to this parifh Veftry an Account of every perfon's land they fhall proceffiion, and the perfons prefent at the Same, and of all land in their precinct they fhall fail to proceffion, and the particular reafon of fuch failure.

Purfuant to an Act of Affembly of this Colony, and in Obedience to an Order of Henrico County Court, made at a Court held for ye County aforefaid, the firft day of December, 1735: The Veftry do order that William Porter, Junr., John Warriner and Stephen Floyd, with the Affiftance of the free holders and Neighbors, do Sometime before the laft day of March Next Coming, goe in proceffion and renew the bounds of all Land from the Weftern Run to the outward precinct on Chickahominy Swamp, and that the faid William Porter, John Warriner and Steven Floyd, (or any two of them,) do take and return to this parifh Veftry An Account of every perfon's land they fhall proceffion, and the perfons prefent at the Same, and of all Land in their precincts they fhall fail to proceffion, and the particular Reafon of Such failure.

Purfuant to an Order of Veftry, made at a Veftry held for Henrico parifh the fixth day of December, ano. Dom. 1735, Directing the proceffioning of every perfon's Land within the faid parifh, The Several proceffioners appointed do make Return of their proceedings within their refpective precincts as follows, viz:

In obedience to this within order we have proceffioned all the Lands within our precinct, Excepting William Adkins, living in Goochland County & never appeared; Thomas Pleafants and Mary Mofby, Orphants, and John Watkins and Ann Daniel, We have returned to the Church Wardens, given under our hands this 18 day of March, 1735.

JOHN WATSON,
JOHN WILLIAMSON,
WILLIAM PATMAN.

Copy Teft.

Proceffioned Obadiah Smith's land, with his Confent, himfelf being prefent.
Proceffioned Mary Cannon's Land, with her Confent.
Proceffioned Gilly Grew Marrin's Land, with his Confent.
Proceffioned Luke Smith's Land, he being prefent.
Proceffioned Jofeph Pleafants' Land, he being prefent.
Proceffioned John Pleafants' Land, he being prefent.
Proceffioned William Hill's Land, he being prefent.
Proceffioned Robert Sharp's Land, he being prefent.
Proceffioned John Britain's Land, he being prefent.
Proceffioned William Ferriffe's Land, he being prefent.
Proceffioned Robert Morriff's Land, he being prefent.
Proceffiioned part of Thomas Williamfon's Line.

By JOELL WALKER,
HENRY STOKES,
JOHN SMITH.

Copy Teft.

Purfuant to an Order of Veftry, held for Henrico parifh ye 6 day of Dec'r. 1735, we have proceffioned the Lands ordered us by the Veftry, which are as followeth, viz: proceffioned the Line of Richard Levens and Benjamin Burton; alfo the line of Benjamin Burton and John Cox; John Cox and John Whitlo's line; John Whitlo's and William Whitlo's line; James Whitlo's and William Whitlo's line; James Whitlo's Back line; Darby Enrufty and John Scott's line; Darby Enrufty and Abraham Childers' line; Larner Bradfhaw and Jofeph Adkins' line; Abraham Childers and Jofeph Adkins' line; Abraham Childers and John Scott's line; Jofeph Adkins, Jane Scott's line; Jane Scott and Frayzer's line; Jofeph Adkins and John Brion's line; John Brion and Frayzer's line; John Brion and Larner Bradfhaw Line; all which Lines we have Renewed in prefence of the parties owning the faid Lands. Alfo we have proceffioned John Cox and Richard Renard Line; And William Whitlo and Richard Renard Line; John Cox and William Whitlo being prefent, and Miell Turpin in behalf of ye faid Renard; alfo we proceffioned the Lines of James and Thomas pleafant's line; William Whitlo and Thomas pleafant's line, Darby Enrufty and Thomas pleafant's line; John and Benj. Scott and Thomas pleafant's Line; all the parties being prefent at the renewing of the bounds aforefaid, (Thomas pleafant only Excepted,) he not having notice. Jofeph Mayo's Land not proceffioned occafioned by his not Attending us there the Time appointed. We also renewed William Burton's Line, Which is all the patiented lands in the precinct. Ordered as per the Veftry above Mentioned.

Teft:

Certified per WM. WHITLO,
JOS. ATKINS.

In Obedience to an Order of the Veftry of this parifh, and according to the directions of an Act of Affembly entitled an Act for Settling the titles and bounds of Land and for preventing unlawful fhooting & Ranging thereupon. We, the Subscribers, having gon in proceffion of the Several Lands within our precinct, as by order dated Dec'r ye 6, 1735, with the freeholders followeth, viz:

Theodric Carter, his Land proceffioned.
John Webb, Do.
Garrard Ellyfon, Do.

John Spear, his land proceffioned
Sam Bugg Do.
Francis Brothers, Do.
Francis Amos, Do.
John Mofs, Do.
William Clarke, Do.
Robert Ferris, Do.
William Ferris, Ju'r, Do.
William Ferris, Sen'r, Do.
Edward Goode, Do.
Ann Auftin, Do.
John Bottom in behalf of
Philamone Smith, Do.
Richard Truman, Jr., Do.
John Bottom, Do.
Richard Truman, Jr, his line not to be found below Boar Swp.
Michael Hartwell, Do.
John Roper, Do.
Thomas Watkins, Do.
Richard More, Do.

Part of John Cock's Land not proceffioned by Reafon of Thomas Pleafants failing to appear. The lines of the Lands between James powel Cocke, and John Robertfon not being found, The lines between James powel Cocke and John Hales not agreed on. John Robertfon, part of his lines not to be found. Edward Moffby refufes to proceffion part of the Land of Thomas Epps, proceffioned in our precinct; the Lines between John Cocke and Giles Carter that is in the County. Given under our hands ye laft day of March, 1736.

Teft:

JNO. COCKE,
GILES CARTER,
GAR'D ELLYSON.

This is to certifie that William Lewis, Henry Hatcher and Daniel Price, with the Affiftance of ye Neighboring freeholders hath renewed all the lines in our precinct according to the Order, Except the line of Jofeph Watfon, which can't be found, and the Land that ye have already Returned to the Church Warden.

Copy Teft:

WILLIAM LEWIS,
DANIEL PRICE,
HENRY HATCHER.

This is to Certifie that we have proceffioned all the Lands in our precinct by me, Thomas Wood, and Jno. Price and Huth's Burton.

This is to Certifie that Edmond Allen, John Faris, Richard Williamfon, with the Affiftance of the Neighboring freeholders, hath renewed all the Lines in our precinct, Except a Line between Capt. James Cocke and Thomas Matthews, and the reafon it was not proceffioned Capt. Cocke never came to proceffion, and a Outline of Jofeph Watfon's, and the reafon that it was not proceffioned, the line could not be found, and every perfon prefent being at the fame time.

January ye 1ft, 1735-6. Proceffioned the following lines Between John Stweed and William Finney; Between William Finney and Judith Cocke. January ye 12, Between Mr. Jofeph Mayo and Wilbfbier Marrien; between Mr. Mayo and James Frankling; Between Thomas Robertfon and Eln'r Williams; Between Mr. Jofeph Mayo and Thomas Robertfon. January ye 15th, Between James Frankling and Thomas Robertfon; Between Thomas Robertfon and William Burton; William Burton and Alex'r Robertfon and Jofeph Mayo; Between Alexander Robertfon and Abram and George Abny. January 16, Between Judith Cocke and Thomas Baily; John Giles and Charles Belew; Between Thomas Baily, John Giles and Charles Belew; Between Nicholas Giles and John Allday. Jan'y 28, Between John Giles, Thomas Mofley; Between Thomas Allday and John Giles. March ye 8th, Between Collo. William Randolph and Francis Marrin. March ye 11th. Between Colo. William Randolph, John Allday, Thos. Mofley. The Lines between Brazner Cocke and Francis Marrin, and between Fran's Marrin and Warham

Eafley, lying obfcure, do agree that the Surveyor fhall run them.

JOHN GILES,
Copy Teft: JOHN ALLDAY.

THE ORDER Executed in proceffioning and returning proceffioned the lines of Martha Hambleton, prefent; William Foard and John Mofley proceffioned John Bowe land, prefent; John Mofby proceffioned William Turner's Land, prefent; David Atkines an John Mofby proceffioned the Land of Will'm Foard, preffent; Mofby and John foard proceffioned the land of John Shepherd, preffent; John Johnfon and James Bohannan. Jacob Shepherd's Land proceffioned, prefent; John Johnfon and John Shepherd proceffioned the Land of Rob't Morris, prefent; Matthew Hutchinson and John Shepherd, David adkin's Land, preffent; William ford and John Mofby proceffioned the Land of Jofeph Parsons, preffent; Robert Mofby and John Brumfield proceffioned William Britain's Land, prefent; Robert Mofley and Henry Britain proceffioned Ifaac Winfton's [13] Land, prefent; Henry Britain and Robert Mofby proceffioned the Land Robert Mofby, prefent; Ifaac Winfton and Henry Britains proceffioned the Land of Ralph Hunt and John Royal, prefent; Robert Mofby and John Whealer proceffioned the Land of Obadiah Smith, prefent; Thomas Conway and James Conway proceffioned the Land of Michael Hilton, prefent; John Whealer, Thomas Conway, Obadiah Smith, proceffioned Matthew Hutchinfon Land, prefent; John Whealer and John Royall proceffioned the Land of Thomas Conway and Nich's Prior, prefent; James Conway and Edward price and Walter Clarke, proceffioned the Land of James Conway and Benjamin Cannon, and Mary Walters, prefent; Thomas Conway and Edward prior and Charles Cannon, proceffioned the Land of Simon Ligon, prefent; William Harler and John Martin proceffioned John Martin's, prefent; Simon Ligon and William Street proceffioned the land of Robert Timfon, prefent; John Tomfon and William Harlow proceffioned the Land of Robert Hardwick, prefent; Thomas Fenton and John North, proceffioned the land of John North, prefent; Robert Hardwick and Edward Tommas, proceffioned Thomas fentons, prefent; William Street and Robert Hardwick proceffioned William Harlo's, prefent; Simon Ligon proceffioned William Street, prefent; John Martin proceff'd Jacob Roberfon, prefent; Charles Cannon and Nich's Prior, proceff'd John Woodfon's Land, prefent, himfelf; proceffioned the land of Abraham Childers, prefent; Hutchins, Burton and Thomas Cottral procefhoned Hutchins Burton's and William Gordins', prefent; Abram Childers and John Gordin, part of a Tract of Collo. William Randolph's not proceff'd. The Lines not found. Thomas Bootwright Not, he being Abfent. Sarah Hews, her Land not proceffioned, No one to fhow us the Lines.

THOS. OWEN,
Copy Teft: WM. BRITAIN,
JOS. PARSONS.

BY VIRTUE of an order of this Veftry of the parifh, We, the Subfcribers, have gon in proceffion and renewed the bounds of all thofe within thofe limits mencioned in the faid order. Several of the Neighboring Free holders, Together with owners of the faid Lands being prefent at the doing of the Same. Thofe under-mencioned Excepted, Viz.: The Several parts of That dividend of Land formerly belonging to John Cocke in the Low grounds, Not done by Reafon none of the owners were prefent when the Adjacent Lands were proceffioned; the Lands whereon Henry Irby lived not done for ye Same Reason. The Line between James powell Cocke and Thomas Pleafants was proceffioned, but in the Meafuring the head Line of the point, Land there was an Error of Thirty poles in the length of that line. The Courfe and diftance is by the faid Cocke and Pleafants agreed on, and between themfelves will rectifie the above Miftake. The Line between James Cocke and William Porter, Junior, Not to be found; and that between the faid Cock and John Williams not done for the Same Reafon. The partition Lines between Between Richard Randolph and Charles Woodfon; alfo that between John Pleafants and the faid Woodfon Omitted by Reafon ye the Said Lines were very plain and well known, Together with Richard Randolph's Not being prefent when the Adjacent Land were proceffioned. The Line between Thos. Pleafants' Land and the Land formerly Benjamin Hatcher's Not don for ye Same Reafon. The bounds of the Land that was Charles Holmes, now John Pleafants, Not don, Neither the upper Nor lower line; the parties Concerned protending to Settle them between them Selves. The Line parting the Land that was formerly Solomon Knibbs and Jas. Hatcher's, not done, there being no line to be found. The head Line of the Said Tract adjoining To Thos. Pleafants', Not done, the parties intending to do it between them Selves. The Line parting the Land of John Bolling, formerly Wm. head's, in like manner to be done.

THOMAS PLEASANTS,
STEPHEN WOODSON,
Copy Teft: CHARLES FLOYD.

We, the Subscribers, have proceffioned all the lines within our precinct, which is betwixt Baly's Run and four Mile Creek, Except the Line betwixt Edward Goode and Edward Bennet, and Bennet refufe to proceffion that Line and A Line betwixt Edward Goode and Thos. Matthis, which they have agreed to make; and a line betwixt Wm. Frogmorton and Edward Bennet, we could not find; and a parcel of Land upon White-oak Swamp, belonging to Mr. Eppes, who never came to meet us tho, Often required; and a Line between Capt. James Cocke and John Williams. Cocke never came tho, required.

By us,

EDWARD GOODE,
SAMUEL S. GATHRIGHT,
Copy Text. JOHN :**** HOBSON.

The lands Between Two mile Creek, four Mile Creek, and the Main Country Road, Quietly proceffioned, Except between John Redford's and William Parker; likewife between Abraham Childers and Henry Sharp, but agree to have the lines run by Maj'r John Bowling Quietly.

ABRAHAM CHILDERS,
JOHN REDFORD, JUN'R,
HENRY SHARP.

We, the Subfcribers, have proceffioned all the Land within our precinct; only the Lands belonging to the honourable William Randolph, Efq'r, and mr. William Randolph, Gent., in Goochland, their Lines Not being found. Collo. Richard Randolph never came to go with us, and his is left undone. Robert Hardwick's, John North's, Thos. Fenton's, George Hardwick, prefent with the Owners thereof; Thomas Ally, Thos. Jennett's, John Shoemaker, prefent; Nich's Pryor, Thomas Cosral, each being one with the other; Jacob Robinfon's, Benjamin Cannon's, Charles Cannon, prefent; George Freeman, John Griffin, Thomas Ally, prefent; part of mr. William Randolph, Gent., in Goochland, being done, which part lies in the Ifland of Tuckahoe; those being part of Several perfon's Land left undone by Reafon of the Gent's Lines as firft Mencioned not being done.

JOHN ELLIS,
May ye 3, 1736. WILL'A ELLIS,
Copy Teft: ABRA. CHILDERS.

The lines between John Cocke and William Parsons, both agreed in the prefence of Giles Carter and Thos. Jolley. The Line between John Cocke and Jofeph Woodfon, proceffioned, and both agreed in prefence of Wm. Porter, Sen'r, John Williams, James Volton. The Line between Joseph Woodfon and William Porter, Jun'r, proceffioned, and both agreed in prefence of William Porter, Sen'r, John Cocke, John Williams, Jane Vaulton. The line between William Porter, Sen'r and Humphrey Smith, proceffioned, and both agreed in prefence of William Porter, Sen'r. The Line between Francis Gathright and Elizabeth Eaft, proceffioned, and both agreed in prefence of William Porter, Sen'r and John Williams. The line between John Cocke and Thomas Watkins, proceffioned, and both agreed in prefence of William Porter, Sen'r. The Line between Thomas Watkins and Jofeph Woodfon, proceffioned, and both agreed in prefence of John Cocke and William Porter, Senior. The Line between William Porter, Sen'r and Thos. Watkins, proceffioned, and both agreed in prefence of John Cocke. The Line between William porter, Sen'r and James Cocke, proceffioned and agreed. The Line between Cols. Harrifon, and William Lewis, and Thomas Watkins, and Thomas Binford, and Edward Mofby, proceffioned, and agreed in prefence of James powel Cocke, John Cocke, Giles Carter, John Owin. The Line between Charles Floyd and Stephen Floyd, proceffioned and agreed. A Line between Stephen Woodfon and William Lewis, proceffioned and agreed. A line between William porter, Sen'r and James Vaulton, agreed. A Line between William Porter, Sen'r, and John Williams, agreed.

The Lines between William Lewis and Thomas Watkins, not renewed, becaufe Thos. Watkins would not appear. a Line between Stephen Floyd and Stephen Woodfon, not agreed on. A Line between Wm. Porter, Senior, and James Cocke, Not renewed, becaufe James Cocke did not appear. Francis Rowins' Line not proceffioned, Nobody would appear to do it for him.

WM. PORTER, JUN'R,
JOHN WORRINER,
Copy Teft: STEPHEN FLOYD.

AT A VESTRY held at Curl's Church, for Henrico parifh, on Sunday, the 18th July, 1736.

Prefent.

William Randolph, Bowler Cocke, John Bolling, James Powell Cocke, James Cocke, John Redford, John Powell, Edward Curd, John Williamfon and William Fuller, Gent. Veftrymen.

The reverend mr. William Stith[14] produces a Letter from the Hon'l William Gooch, Efq'r, his Majesty's Lieut. Governor of the Colony, and another from the rever'd mr. James Blair, Commiffary, directed to the Church Wardens and Gent. of the Veftry, recommending the faid mr. Stith to the Cure of this parifh, which are read, and ye faid Mr. Stith hath this Day performed his minifterial function, both in preaching and reading to the General Satiffaction and approbation of the Veftry, whereupon they do unanimously agree to receive him as Minifter of this parifh.

Signed by

JAMES POWELL COCKE,
JAMES COCKE,
Church Wardens.

Purfuant to an Order of Vestry, held for Henrico parish the 6 day of December, ano. 1735: We, John Stewart, Edward Cox and Benjamin Burton, being appointed proceffioners in the precinct between Cornielioufffe's two Mile Creek and the Mane County road: In obedience to the faid order, we mett on the 9th day of January, and dide proceed to fulfil the faid order, viz.:

The bounds of Land between Edward Cox and John Cox, renewed; the Said Edward and John being present, done in prefence of Thomas Jordan.

As Alfo the Bounds of Land Between Edward Cox and Thos. Jordan, the parties being prefent; renewed in prefence of John Cox.

As Alfo the bounds of land between John Cox and Thos. Jordan, renewed; the partys being prefent.

As Alfo the bounds of land between William perkins and Thomas Branch, renewed, the partys being prefent; done in prefence of Arthur Giles.

As Alfo the Bounds of Land between Thomas Branch and William Burton, renewed, the parties being prefent; done in prefence of William pirkins and Arth'r Giles.

As Alfo the Bounds of Land between William pirkins and William Burton, renewed, the parties being prefent; done in prefence of Tho. Branch and Art. Giles.

As Alfo the Bounds of Land between Edward Cox and William pirkin, renew'd, the partys being prefent; done in prefence of Authur Giles.

As Alfo the bounds of Land between Edward Cox and Sarah Mofley, renewed, the parties being prefent; done in prefence of Wm. Pirkins and Art. Giles.

As Alfo the bounds of land between Sarah Mofly and William pirkins, renewed, the parties being prefent; done in prefence of Art. Giles.

As Alfo the bounds of Land between Thomas Branch and John Taylor, an Orphant, renewed; William pirkins, his Guardian, and the said Branch being prefent; done in prefence of Art. Giles.

As Alfo the bounds of Land between Sarah Mofley and John Taylor, the Said Mofley and William pirkins being prefent at renewing the fame; done in prefence of Arthur Giles and Thomas Pirkins.

As Alfo the bounds of land between William pirkins and John Taylor, renewed, the Said pirkins being prefent; done in prefence of Art. Giles.

As Alfo the bounds of land between William Burton and Samuel Hancock, renewed, the party being prefent; done in prefence of Thomas Woodcocke.

As Alfo the bounds of Land between William pirkins and Samuel Hancock, ye Said pirkins being prefent; done by the Confent of ye Said Hancocke; prefent, Thomas Woodcocke.

As Alfo the Bounds of Land between Wm. Pirkins and Robert Bullington, renewed, the parties being prefent; done in prefence of Thos. Woodcocke.

As Alfo the bounds of land between John Stewart and Judith Cocke, renewed, the partys being prefent; done in prefence of Thos. Ballow, William Finney, Abraham Baly.

As Alfo the bounds of land between Judith Cocke and Tabitha Ballou, renew'd, the partys prefent; done in prefence of Thos. Ballow, Abra. Baly and Wm. Finney.

As Alfo the bounds of land between Abraham Baly and Tabitha Ballou, renewed, the partys being prefent; done in prefence of Thomas Ballow and Wm. Finney.

As Alfo the bounds of land between Benjamin Burton and Wm. Finney, renew'd, the partys being prefent; don in prefence of Abraham Baly and Thomas Ballow.

As Alfo the bounds of land between Wm. Finney and Richard Cox renewed, the partys being prefent; Don in prefence of Abraham Baly.

As Alfo the bounds of land between John Cox and Michael

Turpin, renewed, the parties being prefent; don in prefence of of Hays Whitloe.

As Alfo the bounds of land between John Cox and Benj'a Burton, renewed, the parties being prefent; done in prefence of Hais Whitloe.

As Alfo the bounds of land between William Finney and Michael Turpin, renewed, the parties being prefent; Done in prefence of John Cox and Hays Whitloe.

As Alfo the bounds of land between John Stewart and John Ellis, the faid Stewart prefent; renewed by confent of the faid Ellis, in prefence of Benj. Burton, Junr.

As Alfo the bounds of L'd Between Francis Epps and Thomas Branch, renewed, the parties being prefent; done in prefence of Thos. Branch and Roderick Evans.

As Alfo the bounds of land between Francis Eppes and Will. Burton, renewed, the parties being prefent; don in prefence of Thomas Branch and Roderick Evans.

As Alfo the bounds of Land between Francis Eppes and John Stewart, renewed, the parties being prefent; done in prefence of Roderick Evans.

As Alfo the bounds of land between Francis Eppes and Samuel Hancock, renewed, the said Hancock being prefent; don by ye Confent of ye Sd. Eppes.

As Alfo the bounds of land between Benja. Burton and Samuel Hancock, renewed; the parties being prefent.

As Alfo the bounds of land between Benja. Burton and John Ellis, renewed, the parties being prefent; done in prefence of Abraham Baly.

As Alfo the bounds of land between William Fuller and Hays Whitloe, renewed, the Said Whitloe being prefent; don by Confent of the Said Fuller, in the prefence of Wm. Finney.

As Alfo the bounds of land between William Fuller and prudence Cox, renewed by Confent of the Said Fuller, in prefence of Wm. Finney and Hays Whitloe.

As Alfo the bounds of land between Robert Bullington and Thos. Jordan, renewed; the parties being prefent.

As Alfo the bounds of land between William pirkins and Thomas Jordan, renewed, the Said Jordan being prefent; don by Confent of the said pirkins in prefence of Robert Bullington.

An Account of Lands not proceffioned, with the particular reafons why they were not proceffioned.

The bounds of land between Edward Cox and John Cox at a place Call'd Wilkinfon's Bottom, not renewed; the parties being prefent and Willing to proceffion, but no line to be found.

The bounds of land between William Randolph and Edward Cox, not renewed, by reafon of the faid Randolph's failing to come to renew the Same.

The bounds of land between William Randolph and Thomas Jordan, not renewed, by reafon of the faid Randolph's failing to come to renew the fame.

The bounds of land between William Randolph and Robert Bullington, not renewed, by reafon of the faid Randolph's failing to come.

The bounds of land between William Randolph and Roderick Urquhart, not renewed, by reafon of both parties Abfence.

The bounds of land between William Randolph and William parker, not renewed, by reafon of the Said Randolph's failing to come to renew the Same.

The bounds of land between William Randolph and the Gleeb Land, not renewed, by reafon of the Said Randolph's failing to come to renew the Same.

The bounds of land between Maj'r John Bolling and the Gleeb Land not renewed, by reafon No perfon to Sho the Bounds.

The bounds of land between Maj'r John Bolling and Temperance Bullington, not renewed, by reafon of the Said Bullington's Abfence.

The bounds of land between Robert Bullington and Roderick Urquhart, not renew'd, by reafon of the said Urquhart's Abfence.

The bounds of land between Capt. Francis Eppes and Benja. Burton, not renew'd; the parties prefent and Willing to proceffion, but no limits be found.

The bounds of land between Capt. Francis Eppes and Wm.

Fuller, Not renewed, by reafon of the Said Eppes failing to Come to renew the fame.

The bounds of land between Capt. Francis Eppes and John Cox, not renewed, by reafon of the Said Eppes failing to come to renew the Same.

The bounds of land between Maj'r John Bolling and Capt. Francis Eppes, not renewed, by reafon of both parties being Abfence.

The bounds of land between Majr. John Bolling and William Fuller, not renewed, by reafon of both partys' Abfence.

The bounds of land between Prudence Cox and Richard Renard, not renewed, by reafon of both partys' Abfence.

The bounds of land between William Finney and Abra. Baily, not renewed, the party's prefent and Willing to proceffion, but no line to be found.

The bounds of land between William Finney and Judith Cocke, not renewed. The partys prefent and Willing to proceffion, but no line to be found.

JOHN STEWART,
EDWARD COX,
Copy Teft: BENJA. BURTON.

AT A VESTRY held at Curl's Church, for laying the parifh Levey, the Eleventh day of December, 1736.

Prefent.

JAMES POWELL COCKE,
JAMES COCKE, GENT., } *Church Wardens.*

William Randolph, Efqr., Richard Randolph, John Redford, Bowler Cocke, John powell and William Fuller, Gent. Veftrymen.

Henrico Parifh, Dr., 1736.

	Gr. Tob.	Cafk.
To Ballance due to Collector laft year,	175	
To the Rev'd mr. William Stith,	12,000	480
To Conveniency on Do.	2,031	

To Sackvil Brewer, Reader, a year's Sallary,	2,000	80
To Do. Clerk of the Veftry,	1,000	40
To John Eals, Reader at Chapel,	2,000	80
To John Hobfon, Sexton,	600	24
To Elenor Williams, Sexton at Chapel,	600	24
To the Church Wardens for Communion Bread and Wine,	400	
To Sufanna Woodcocke for keeping her Son,	1,200	40
To Mary North for keeping Sufanna Burnet,	1,000	40
To Hutchins Burton for keeping Sufanna Rollings,	700	28
To the Collector for Infolvents, &c., perfons twice lifted.	891	
To the Rev'd Mr. Brooks for fhort Levy'd him laft year for preaching,	680	
To Robert Hardwick for his Son, an impotent perfon,	500	
To Elizabeth Fuffel for Keeping and Burying Elenor Weft,	600	
To the Collectors for a Miftake in levying mr. Gavin's Tob'o laft year,	351	
Cafk,	844	
	27,572	
Commiffion on 27,572 ℔ Tobacco at 6 per Cent, is	1,654	
	29,226	
Due from the Collectors to the parifh,	543	
Henrico Parifh is Credit 1736,	29,769	

By the Collectors for 14 per Cent. of 4,136 ℔ Tob'o Receiv'd of Dale parifh, and by him paid here with that Deduction,	579
By 973 Tithables, at 30 ℔ Tobacco per pole, is	29,190
	29,769

John Nafh, Gent., is Appointed Collector of this parifh this year, and it is ordered that he do receive of every Tithable perfon within the faid parifh according to law. Thirty pounds of Tobacco being the Levy for this year, and if any perfon refufes to pay the Same, he is to Deftrain for it, and that he do pay unto each parifh Creditor Refpectively their Several Sums of Tobacco, as in the proportions of the faid levy are mentioned, for the performance of all which the faid John Nafh Enters into Bond; Richard Randolph and Bowler Cocke, Gent., Enters themfelves Security.

John Nafh, Gent., prefents an Account of the Money received by him as Collector at Six pence per pole of the Tithables in this parifh, which was to have been apply'd towards the repairing the Chapel, by which it appears that there is due from him to the parifh the Sum of Nineteen pounds Two Shillings and Two pence. It is ordered that he do pay the faid Sum of Money to Richard Randolph, Gent., who is defired to receive and keep the Same in his hands for the ufe of the parifh till further Orders.

JAMES POWELL COCKE, }
JAMES COCKE, } *Ch. Wardens.*

AT A VESTRY held at Curl's Church for Henrico parifh, ye 8th day of October, Anno. Dom., 1737, for laying ye parifh Levey.

Prefent.

James powell Cocke, James Cocke, Church Wardens; Richard Randolph, John Redford, Bowler Cocke, John Bolling, William Fuller, John povall, Edward Curd, John Williamfon and Robert Mofby, Gent. Veftrymen.

Henrico Parifh, Dr., for ye year 1737.

	Gr. Tob.	Cafk.
To the Rev'd Mr. William Stith,	10,000	400
To ye 14 per Cent. on Do. for Conveniency,	1,693	
To Sackvil Brewer, Reader at Curl's Church,	2,000	80
To Do. as Clerk of ye Veftry,	500	20
To John Ales, Reader at Chapel,	2,000	80

To John Hobfon, Sexton at Curl's Church,	600	24
To Elenor Williams, Sexton at Chapel,	600	24
To ye Church Wardens for Communion Bread and Wine,	400	
To Sufanna Woodcock for keeping her Son, an Impotent perfon,	1,200	48
To Mary Burnet for keeping Sufanna Burnnet,	1,000	40
To Hutchins Burton for keeping Sufanna Rollings,	700	28
To Robert Hardwick for keeping his Son, an Impotent perfon,	500	20
To ye Collector for Insolvents, &c.,	330	
To the Church Wardens for ye Ufe of Elizabeth Baily, a poor Old Woman,	400	
To the Church Wardens for ye Ufe of Widow Stephens, a poor Blind Woman,	600	
To 14 per Cent. on faid 1,000 for Conveniency,	160	
To Edmond Allen for keping his Son, an Ideot,	600	
To Elizabeth Fuffel for keeping John Weft, an Infant,	400	
To Thos. Jennet, for keeping Eliza. pike, till laying ye Next Levey,	900	
	24,583	764
Cafk,	764	
	25,347	
To Commiffion at 6 per Cent on 25,347, is	1,520	
	26,867	
To 5,250 ℔ Groff Tob'o to be appli'd towards Building ye New Church at Williamfon's	5,250	
To 5,250 ℔ Grofs Tob'o to be Apply'd towards Building and Repairing of Gleeb Houfes,	5,240	
Per Contra Cr.,	37,367	
By Ballance due from Collector laft year,	543	
By 1,050 Tithables at 35 per pole, Amounts to	35,750	
By a Ballance due to the Collector,	74	
	37,267	

William ffuller, Gent., is appointed Collector of the parifh Levey for this year, and it is ordered that he do receive of every Tithable perfon within the Said parifh, Thirty-two pounds of Tobacco, with the Ufual deduction being the Levey for this year, and if any perfon refufes to pay the Same, he is to Deftrain for it; and that he do pay unto each parifh Creditor refpectively, their Several and refpective Sums of Tobacco as in the Said Levey appears to be Due; for the performance of all which the faid ffuller enters into Bond; John Redford and John Povall Securitys.

On the Motion of Thomas Jennet, his Son Robert is Exempted from paying parifh Levey.

It is ordered that Richard Randolph, Gent., do pay James Cocke, Church Warden, Two pounds one Shilling and Nine pence out of the parifh Money in his hands, for Somuch by the Said Cocke, paid James Hunt for Mending ye Chappel Windows.

The Veftry do agree to build a Church on the Moft Convenient place at or near Thomas Williamfon's in this parifh, to be Sixty feet in length and Twenty-five feet in breadth, and fourteen feet pitch; to be finifhed in a plain Manner, after the Moddle of Curl's Church. And it is ordered that the Clerk do set up Advertifements of the particular parts of the faid buildings, and of the time and place of undertaking the Same.

It is ordered that the Collector do receive of every Tithable perfon in the parifh, five pounds of Tobacco, after the Ufual deduction, to be Apply'd towards building the New Church at Williamfon's.

It is ordered that the Collector do receive of every Tithable perfon in this parifh, five pounds of Tobacco after the Ufual Deductions; to be Apply'd towards building and repairing the Gleeb Houfes. Richard Randolph, Gent., is appointed to treat with fome perfon to undertake ye faid reparations, &c.

Signed, JAMES POWELL COCKE,
JAMES COCKE,
Ch. Wardens.

AT A VESTRY held at Curl's Church for laying the Levey of Henrico parifh, Nov. 25th, 1738.

Prefent.

the Rev'd William Stith, Jas. powell Cocke, James Cocke, Bowler Cocke, John Bolling, John Redford, William ffuller and John Povall, Gent. Veftrymen.

Dr. Henrico Parifh, Nov'r 25th, 1738.

	Gr. Tob.	Cafk.
To the Rev'nd Mr. William Stith, a year's Sallerry,	16,000	640
To 14 per Cent. for Conveniency,	2,708	
To a balla. due to Collector,	74	
To Jack Brewer, Reader at Curl's,	2,000	80
To Do., his Sallery as Clerk at Veftry,	500	20
To John Eals, Reader at Chappel,	2,000	80
To John Hobfon, Sexton at Curl's,	600	24
To Elenor Williams, Sexton at Chappel,	600	24
To the Church Wardens for bread and Wine,	400	
To Sufanna Woodcocke for keeping and burying her Son,	228	
To Mary North for Keeping Mary Burnet,	1,000	40
To Hutchings Burton for Keeping Sufanna Rollins 6 Months,	364	
To Robert Hardwick, for Keeping his Son,	500	20
To the Church Wardens for ye Ufe of Elizabeth Baley,	400	
To 14 per Cent. for Conveniency,	65	
To the Church Wardens for the Ufe of Widow Stephen's Net, 1,000, is	1,162	
To Elizabeth Morton for burying John Armftead,	200	
To the Church wardens for Rebeckah pruit,	520	
To the Collector for Infolvents and perfons twice lifted,	700	
To Edmond Allen for Keeping his Son,	600	24
To the Church Wardens for John Weft and Infant,	400	16

To Thos. Jennet for Keeping John pike, an Infant, till laying next parifh levy,	900	35
To James Hatcher for making benches at Church, 120 is	139	
	32,060	1,012
Cafk Added,	1,012	
	33,072	
To Commiffion on 34656 at 6 p. Ch. is	2,079	
	35,151	

Henrico parifh Credit.

By 1,83 Tithables at 32 ℔ Tobo. per pole is	34,656
" Ballance due to the Collector,	495
	35,151

James Cocke, Gent. Church Warden, produfeth his Account of Two pounds two Shillings and Eleven pence, Current Money, by him paid for repairs done this Chappel. It is ordered that Richard Randolph, Gent., do pay him the faid fum out of his parifh Money in his hands.

James powell Cocke produfeth his Account againft the parifh, wherein it appears that Eight Shillings, Current Money, is due to him for Mending the Church Windows. It is ordered that Richard Randolph, Gent., do pay him the Same out of the parifh Money in his hands.

Mr. William ffuller is appointed a Collector of the parifh Levey this year, and it is ordered that he do receive of every Tithable perfon in the Said parifh, thirty-two pounds of Tobo. according to Law, and that he pay the Several Allowances Above Mentioned to the refpective perfons to whom it is due. Bowler Cocke and John Poval, Gent., enter themfelves Securitys.

JAMES POWELL COCKE,
JAMES COCKE.

AT A VESTRY held at Curl's Church, for henrico parifh, July ye 21ft, Ano. Dom. 1739:

Prefent.

The Rever'd William Stith, James powell Cocke, James Cocke, Bowler Cocke, John Redford, Edward Curd, Robert Mofby, John Povall, William ffuller and John Williamfon, Gent.

In obedience to an Order of Henrico Court, and purfuant to an Act of Affembly of this Colony, the Veftry do proceed to divide the parifh into Several precincts and appoint perfons to go in proceffion and renew the Bounds of Lands according to law.

firft precinct.

Purfuant to an Act of Affembly of this Colony, and in obedience to an Order of Henrico Court, it is Ordered that John North, Thomas ffenton and Thomas Ellis, with the affiftance of their Neighboring free holders, do Sometime before the laft day of March next, go in proceffion and renew the Bounds of all Lands from the Mouth of Weft Ham to William Gorden's, hence upwards, all between Gorden's Road and James River to the head of the parifh. And that the said John North, Thomas ffenton, and Thomas Ellis (or any two of them) do take and return to this parifh Veftry an Account of every perfons Land by them proceffioned, together with the names of thofe prefent, and Alfo what Lands they fhall fail to proceffion and the particular Reafon of Such failure.

Second precinct.

ffrom William Gorden's Road to the head of the parifh, thence to the Main Road Swamp, thence down to Turner's Run, thence up Hungry Branch to the head of Upland Brook, from thence to Gorden's aforefaid. John Shepherd, John Royal and Robert Webb are appointed proceffioners.

Third precinct.

All between Chickahominy Swamp and Upland Brook, to the head of the faid Brook. Nathaniel Bacon, John Watkins and peter patrick are appointed proceffioners.

Col. Wm. Byrd, Jr.,
who donated the site upon which St. John's Church stands.

ffourth precinct.

All between Chickahominy Swamp and the Brook Road, as low as Mary Cannon's and Smith's Mill. Robert Sharp, John pleafant and John Brittain are appointed proceffioners.

ffifth precinct.

All between the Mouth of Gilley's Creek and Weft Ham, on the River, and to extend back from Gorden's and Mary Cannon's. John Coles, James Young and Richard Levens are appointed proceffioners.

Sixth precinct.

ffrom the Mouth of Gilley's Creek on James River to William Lewis's, on Chickahominy Swamp, thence upward as high as Smith's Mill and Mary Cannon's. Thom's Watkins, John Harwood and Alex'r Mofs, proceffioners.

Seventh precinct.

All below the Mouth of Gilley's Creek and Corneliuf's, on James River, and to Extend back as far as Seven pines Road, and as low as the Southern Branch Bridge. ffrans. Redford, Gilly Marrin and George Abney are proceffioners.

Eigth precinct.

All between Corneliuf's and Two Mile Creek, on the River, and to Extend back as far as the Main Country Road. Sam'l Hancock, William parker and John Cox are appointed proceffioners.

Ninth precinct.

All between Two Mile Creek, ffour Mile Creek, James River and the Main Country Road. Ifaac Sharp, William perce and William Stone are appointed proceffioners.

Tenth precinct.

All between Corneliuf's and four Mile Creek, on the Main Road, hence back as far as the Seven pines Road. John ffrafer, James Whitlow and John Whitlow are proceffioners.

Eleventh precinct.

All between William Lewis's, Boar Swamp, Chickahominy Swamp, and the Seven pines Road. Joseph Watfon, Martin Martin and Jofeph Childers are appointed proceffioners.

Twelfth precinct.

ffrom the Mouth of Boar Swamp, on Chickahominy, to the lower Bounds of the parifh, thence between Boar Swamp and the parifh line South Wards as far as where the Road forks for Long Bridge and Bottom Bridge. Thomas Watkins, Sam. Bugg and John Carter are proceffioners.

Thirteenth precinct.

ffrom Bayly's Run to four Mile Creek, all between the Road that leads from four Mile Creek Bridge to Chickahominy Swamp and James River. Jofeph Hopfon, Nich's Hopfon and John Darby are appointed proceffioners.

Fourteenth precinct.

All between Bailey's Run and the Lower Bounds of this Parifh, to Extend back as far as the Weftern Run. Charles Woodfon, James Hatcher and John Williams are proceffioners.

ffifteenth precinct.

All between the Weftern Run, the head of Bailey's Run and the parifh line, to Extend North w'd as far as the fork of Long Bridge Road. Humphrey Smith, Thomas Binford and Edward Eaft, proceffioners.

William Randolph, Efqr., who was a Veftryman for the parifh, having resigned that place, Peter Randolph,[15] Gent., is chofen to fucceed him.

It is Ordered the Church Wardens do give Notice an Set up Advertifements at all publick places in this parifh, that on the Second Thursday in October next, At Curl's Church, will be held a Veftry, in order to let out the Building of the New Church, at which time, the parifh levy will be laid.

JAMES POWEL COCKE,
JAMES COCKE,
Church Wardens.

AT A VESTRY, held for Henrico parifh, the xj day of October, Anno que Dom. 1739:

Prefent.

Richard Randolph, Bowler Cocke, John Williamfon, John Bolling, Edward Curd, Robert Mofby, James Powell Cocke, James Cocke, John Povall and Wm. ffuller, Gent., Veftry-men.

Wm. ffuller, late Collector of this parifh, on Account of parifh Tob'o, by him Sold in the Year 1738, viz:

		£.	s.	d.
To the Honb'le William Randolph, Efq.	2,915@12 per ct. amounting to	17	9	9½
To Mr. Beverley Randolph,	1,164@13 do.	7	11	3¾
To Richard Randolph, Gent.	3,978@1⅓ do.	24	7	4½
and 432 Accounted for by faid Collector,	@1⅓ do.	2	14	0
		52	12	5¾

Richard Randolph, Gent., produfes an Account for Buildings and repairs done on the Glebe, by which it appears that a Balance of thirty-nine pounds eight fhillings and eight pence, current Money, is due to him from the parifh. It is thereupon Ordered, that the feveral fums of Money, which appears by this collection account, due to the parifh, viz: from Honourable William Randolph, Efqr., Seventeen pounds Nine Shillings and Nine pence half; from Mr. Beverley Randolph, Seven pounds Elleven Shillings and three pence, three farthings; and from the faid Collector, Mr. William ffuller, two pounds fourteen Shillings. Amounting in the whole to twenty Seven pounds fifteen Shillings and a peny farthing—be paid unto the faid Richard Randolph in part of this Ballance.

The Veftry proceed to Lay the parifh Levy:

Debtor Henrico parifh, for the year 1739.

	Gr. Tob'o.	Cafk.
To the Rev'd Mr. Stith, 16,640 Net is	17,708	640
To Ballance due to laft year's Collector,	495	
To Sackville Brewer, Reader at Curl's,	2,000	80
To ditto, Clerk of the Veftry, being proceffioning year,	1,000	40
To John Eals, Reader at Chapel,	2,000	80
To John Hobfon, Sexton at Curle's,	600	24
To Elenor Williams, Sexton at Chapel,	600	24
To the Church Wardens, for Communion Bread and Wine,	400	
To ditto, for the ufe of Mary Burnet, if living,	1,000	
To ditto, for the ufe of Elizabeth Baley,	400	
To ditto, for Rebecca pruet, neet 600 is	698	
To Edmond Allen, for keeping his Son, an Idiot,	600	24
To Robert Hardwick, for keeping his Son,	500	
To the Church Wardens, for the ufe of John Weft, an Infant,	400	16
To ditto, for the ufe of Jane Jennings,	800	32
To ditto, for the ufe of Mary Hutchens,	800	
To So much towards Building the New Church, 20,000 Neet is	23,256	
Tobacco Levied to Build Barn on the Glebe, 5,000 Neet is	5,816	
	60,073	960
Cafk added,	960	
	61,033	
Com's at 6 per ct. on 69,544, the Whole Sum to be received,	4,172	
	65,205	
Ballance due,	499	
	65,704	

Henrico Parifh, Cr.

By William Fuller, late Collector as per his own Account,	96
By 1,112 Tithables at 59 ℔ Tob'o per pole is	65,608
	65,704

Sackville Brewer is appointed Collector of the parifh for the enfuing year, and it is ordered that he do receive of every Tithable perfon within the faid parifh, the fum of Fifty Nine pounds of Tobacco, after the Ufual Deduction, and that he do pay the Several Allowances above mentioned to the perfons to whom due. Bowler Cocke and Beverley Randolph, Gent.[16] Enter themfelves Securitys for the Same.

Signed: JAMES POWELL COCKE,
JAMES COCKE,
Churc Wardens.

AT A VESTRY held for Henrico parifh, on the Twentieth day of Dec'r, anno 1739:

Prefent.

Mr. William Stith, Minifter; James Powel Cock and James Cocke, Church Wardens; Richard Randolph, John Redford, James Povall, James Williamfon, William ffuller and Robert Mofby, Gent., Veftrymen.

It is agreed that a Church be Built on the Moft Convenient Spot of Ground near ye Spring, on Richardfon's Road, on the South Side of Bacon's Branch, on the Land of the Honourable William Byrd, Efqr., to be Sixty feet long and Twenty five broad, and fourteen feet pitch'd, to be finifh'd in a plain manner after the moddle of Curl's Church. Richard Randolph, Efq., Gent., undertakes the faid Building, and engages to finifh the Same by the Tenth day of June, which fhall be in the year of our Lord Seventeen hundred and forty one; for which the Veftry agrees to pay him the fum of three hundred and seventeen pounds Ten Shillings Current Money, to be paid by the Ammount of Sales of twenty thoufand pounds of Tob'o Annually, to be Lev'd on the parifh and fold here for money, till the whole payment be compleat. It is agreed that a Barn be Built on the Glebe forty feet long and Twenty broad and Ten and a half feet pitch'd, the frames to be Sawed out of Good timber to be covered in good heart fhingles, nailed on; the floor to be laid with two inch plank, and Underpined with Brick or Stone. James Hatcher undertakes the faid Building, and engages to finish the fame Workmanlike, by the Twentieth day of June next, for which the Veftry agrees to pay him Thirty five pounds Current Money, to be Raifed by the fale of Tobacco Levy'd on the parifh for that purpofe.

It is ordered that the parifh Collector do pay into the hands of the Church Wardens the Tobacco levyed for the ufe of the parifh, as foon as he can Conveniently Collect the fame, and the Church Wardens are Impowered to make any private Bargain and fell the faid Tobacco for money, but not under twelve fhillings and fix pence per hundred, otherwife they are to fell it at publick fale to the higheft bidder.

JAMES POWELL COCKE,
JAMES COCKE.

Every perfon under Writen, have proceffioned their land Marks as us.

Richard More, Richard Truman, Michael Hartfield, Thomas Bottom, ffrancis Wilkinfon, ffrans. Brothers, ffrancis Wagftaff, Thomas Watkins, John Hales, John Speare, Genet Ellifon, Samuel Bugg, Ann Auftin, Edward Goode, John Ferris, William Ferris, William Clark, Robert fferris, John Cocke, Walter Leigh.

Certified by us,

THOMAS WATKINS,
SAMUEL BUGG,
JOHN CARTER,
JAS. POWELL COCKE,
Teft: JAMES COCKE.

Purfuant to the within order, we, the fubfcribers, have made quiet and peaceable proceffion of all lands according to the within orders, except two Certain parcels belonging to

Orphants not of Age—one being left by Jofeph Pleafants, deceafed, and the other by Jofeph Mofby, dec'd.

Per NATH'L BACON, JOHN WATKINS,
PETER PATRICK.
JAS. POWELL COCK,
Teft: JAMES COCKE.

This is to Certifye, that we have proceffioned the Lands within our Bounds according to order, with peaceable pof-feffion, and Satisfaction to the perfons whose names are fub-fcribed: Between & William Porter, Sen'r, Humphrey Smith, William Porter, Jr., John Pleafant, John Cock, William Perfons, Thos. Watkins, William Shields, Charles Floyd, Stephen Floyd, Stephen Woodfon, John Midleton, Geo. Pike, Thomas Binford, Foliot Power, Wm. Eaft.

HUMPHREY SMITH, EDWARD EAST,
THOMAS BINFORD.
March 29th, 1740.
JAMES POWELL COCKE,
Copy teft: JAS. COCKE.

Feb. 11, 1740—an Account of proceffioning, viz: phillemon perkins, John Frayfer, William Stone, John Frayfer, Will. Negro, Ben. Scott, Henry Whitloe, Hays Whitloe, Robert Scott, all prefent. Francis Redford, John Redford, Sen'r, prefent. Abraham Childer, John Redford, Sen'r, Jofeph Woodfin, Robert Blairs, Ifaac Sharp, Fran's Rowan, prefent. Fran's previce, Maj John Bolling, John Redford, Jun'r, both prefent, In Obedience to an order of Veftry, for the sub-fcribers have proceffioned all the Lands in our precinct by us.

ISAAC SHARP, WM. PERCE, WM. STONE.
JAS. POWELL COCKE,
Copy Teft: JAMES COCKE.

In Obedience to an Order of Henrico Court, John Whit-loe, James Whitloe and John Frayfer, being appointed by the Veftry of Henrico parifh to procefs and renew the Lands Marks from Four Mile Creek to Cornelius Creek on the Main

Road, and to Extend Back as far as the Seven pines Road, hath renewed them as followeth, Feb. 6, 1739:

The Land Marks between Charles Caffy and philemon Frayfer Renew'd; Charles Caffy and William Frayfer being prefent. The land Mark between Jofeph Adkins and philemon Frayfer renewed; Joseph Adkins, William Frayfer and Charles Caffy being prefent. The land Marks between Charles Caffy and Jofeph Adkins Renewed; Jos. Adkins, Charles Caffy and William Frayfer prefent. The Land marks between Jofeph Adkins and William Frayfer renewed; Jofeph Adkins, Charles Caffy and William Frayfer prefent. The land marks between Benjamin Scot and Jean Scot renewed; Joseph Adkins, Benjamin Scot and Jean Scot prefent. The land marks between Darby Enroughty and Benjamin Scot renewed; Darby Enroughty and Benjamin Scot prefent. The land marks between Henry Whitloe and Benjamin Scot renewed; Henry Whitloe and Benja. Scott prefent. The land marks between Larner Bradfhaw and Charles Caffy renewed; Larner Bradfhaw, Charles Caffy & Henry Whitlo prefent. The land marks between Abraham Childers and Larner Bradfhaw renewed; Larner Bradshaw, Abraham Childers and Charles Caffy prefent. The Landmarks between Abraham Childers and Joseph Adkins renewed; Abraham Childers, Jos. Adkins, Charles Caffy prefent. The landmarks between Abraham Childers and Jean Scot ren'd; Abraham Childers, Jean Scot and Henry Whitloe prefent. The land marks between Abram Childers and Benjamin Scot renew; Abraham Childers, Benja. Scot and Jofeph Adkins prefent. The land marks between Abraham Childers and Darby Enroughty renewed; Abraham Childers, Darby Enroughty and Jofeph Adkins prefent. The land marks between Darby Enroughty and Henry Whitloe renewed; Darby Enroughty, Henry Whitloe and Benja. Scot prefent. The land marks between Benjamin Burton and John Weft renewed; Benjamin Burton, John Weft and Henry Whitloe prefent. The land marks between John Whitloe and John Weft renewed; John Whitloe, John Weft and William Whitloe pref't. The land marks between William Whitloe and John Weft renewed; William Whitloe, John Weft and Miel Turpin prefent. The land mark between

William Whitloe and John Whitloe renewed; William Whitloe and John Whitloe prefent. The landmarks between Wm. Whitloe and Richard Renyard renew'd; William Whitloe and Miles Turpin prefent. The land marks between William Whitloe and Henry Whitloe renew'd; William Whitloe prefent. The land marks between William Whitloe and Henry Whitloe renewed, and James Whitloe renewed; William Whitloe prefent. The land marks bet. James Whitloe and Henry Whitloe renewed; Jas. Whitloe and Wm. Whitloe and Jos. Adkins prefent. The land marks between William Burton, Sen'r, and Benj. Burton renewed; Benja. Benjamin Burton prefent. The landmarks of James Whitloe renewed, binding on unpatent land; William Whitlo and Jofeph Adkins prefent. The land marks between John Weft and Jofeph Richard Reynard not found; and Mr. Jos. Mayo's land marks not renewed; he not coming to the appointed Time. William Burton, Sen'r, land marks not renewed; he not coming to the appointed Time. They both joining to unpatented lands.

Per JAMES WHITLOE, JOHN FRAYSER,
JAS. POWELL COCKE,
Copy Test. JAMES COCKE.

In Obedience to the within order, we have gon in proceffion and renewed the bounds of the Several Tracts of Land within the Limits of the fame Order, in the prefence and with the Confent of the proprietors of faid Lands. Wit. our hands this 15 day of February, 1739.

Per ROBERT SHARP, JNO. PLEASANTS.
JNO. BRITTIAN,
JAS. POWELL COCKE,
Copy Teft. JAMES COCKE.

purfuant to an order of Veftry, we, the fubfcribers, have attempted to renew the Bounds of Mr. John Cocke and Mr. Samuel Wortham's Land, who refufed, for which reafon Mr. Cock, Saith Thos. Carter, Jun'r, and Thos. Cocke, Sen'r, and George Baker, who joins him, Clames part of his Land,

and Mr. Wortham Land not proceffioned, he entending to Survey, &c. Certify'd by us,

THOS. WATKINS, SAM'L BUGG, JOHN CARTER,
JAMES POWELL COCKE,
Copy Teft. JAMES COCKE.

In Obedience to the within Order, we have renewed the Bounds of all ye Lands within mentioned, in peace and quietnefs, with Confent of the Owners. Given under our hands, this 31st day of March, 1740.

JOHN ROYAL, JOHN SHEPHERD, ROB'T WEBB,
JAMES POWELL COCKE,
Copy Teft. JAMES COCKE.

Jofeph Watfon and Jofeph Childers hath feen Richard Williamfon's Land processioned, and Martin Martin's Land proceffioned, and Edward Allen's land proceffioned, and Elizabeth Mottherwiler's land, all but one line between Capt. James Cocke and her, we cant find, and Charles Winfrey's land proceffioned; Thomas Eaft's land proceffioned, and Jofeph Childers' land proceffioned; Capt. James Cock, his land not proceffioned, we cant find any line; Elizabeth Morton, her land not proceffioned, for we cant find any line between Capt. James Cock and her; Thos. Elmore, one Tract of land not proceffioned, we cant find any line; the land where he lives is proceffioned; John Ferris, his land proceffioned.

JAMES POWELL COCKE,
Copy Teft. JAMES COCKE.

In Obedience to an order of Henrico Court, 1739, We, the appointed proceffioners, have, with our utmoft care, proceffioned all the lands within our precinct, Except Some lines not found Agreed on by the Owners thereof, viz: Between Edward Goode and Jefeph pleafants; Edward Goode and Thomas Childrey; Wm. Eaft and Ephraim Gathrit; Thomas Binford and Edward Mofby. Wit's our hands, March 26, 1740.

NICHOLAS HOBSON, JNO. ENROUGHTY,
JAMES POWELL COCKE,
Copy Teft. JAMES COCKE.

Land proceffioned by Thomas Fenton, Thomas Ellis and John North, 1739; Widow Freeman, Holy Freeman, John Do., Amos Hix, (Holy Freeman, John Do., Thomas Ally,) Thomas Jennet, Thomas Ellus, William Ellis, Edward Reves, Wm. Ellis, (bought of Edward Reves, Thomas Ally, Edward Reves, John Shoemaker, Thomas Ally, Wm. Ellis, Thomas Jennet, John Shoemaker, Edward Reves, Edward Reves, Thomas Cottrell, Sam'l Pincham, Thomas Cotrall, Edward Reves, Thomas Cotrall, Jacob Robertfon, Thomas Cotrall, Abra. Childers, Thomas Cotrall, Jacob Robertfon, Richard Cottrall, Thomas Cottrall, Ben. Cannon, Thomas Cottrall, Richard Eaft, Jacob Robertfon, Thos. Cotrall, Nich. Pryor, Thos. Cotrall, Zachariah Ford, Thos. Cotrall, Robert Hardwick, John North, Robert Hardwick, George Chambers, Thos. Fenton, George Chambers; Mr. William Randolph, could not poffibly go over his line; Colo. Richard Randolph, his line not gon over; John Ellis, William Ellis, Thomas Ellis, Hen. Ellis, Charles Ellis, Jofeph Ellis—they all present.

JAMES POWELL COCKE,
Copy Teft. JAMES COCKE,

January 1ft, 1740. In Obedience to an order of Veftry, held for Henrico parifh the 21ft day of July, 1739, we, the fubfcribers, have Been in proceffion and renewed the Bounds of the following lands, viz: The Line Between Gillegrew Morrin and Capt. Jofeph Mayo, the uper Side Capt. Mayo's land; alfo the line between the faid Robertfon and William Burton, Jun'r. The Line betwen Capt. Jos. Mayo and Jas. Franklin. The line between the faid Mayo and Widow Abney, and between the faid Mayo and Gilley Marrin.

prefent—Capt. Jofeph Mayo, Wm. Burton, jr., Thos. Robertfon, James Franklin, George Robertfon.

Per GILLIE MARRIN,
GEORGE, ABNY.

The Line between John Stewart and William Finney. The line between the faid Finney and Capt. Wm. Cocke, dec'd; and between the faid Cocke and Thomas Bailey. prefent—Wm. Finney, John Stewart, Sam'l Branch, Thomas Baley.

The line between the faid Cocke and Tabithy Ballou. prefent—Charles Ballou and Thos. Baley. The line between Thos. Bayley and John Giles. prefent—John Giles and Thos. Mofby. The line between the Said Giles and Thos. Mofby. prefent—John Giles and Thomas Mofby. The line between Frans. Redford and John Allday. prefent—the faid Allday and his two Sons, John and Thomas Allday. The line between Thomas Mofby and Peter Randolph, and between the faid Randolph and John Allday; alfo the line between the faid Randolph and Brazure Cock, and between the faid Randolph and Gilley Marrin; the faid Randolph agreeing that John Alday and Thos. Mofby fhould Show us all his lines who were prefent.

April 1ft, 1740.

FRANCIS REDFORD, GILLIGREW MARRIN,
JAMES POWELL COCKE,
Copy Teft. JAMES COCKE.

In Obedience to an order, Directed to us, the Subfcribers, dated the 21ft day of July, 1739, by the Veftry of Henrico parifh, to proceffion and renew the Bounds of all lands between the mouth of Gilley's Creek and Weftham, on the river, and to Extend back as far as Gordons and Mary Cannons, to which we make the following returns, this 31ft day of March, 1740: We proceffioned all the lands within the Above mentioned Bounds but Colo. William Byrd's and Gilley Marrin's; they, nor no perfons for them, did meet at the Time appointed; they perfons that owned the lands Seemed all Well Satiffied.

Per JOHN COLES, RICHARD LEVENS,
JAMES POWELL COCKE,
Copy Teft. JAMES COCKE.

Purfuant to an Order of Veftry, we, the fubfcribers, have proceffioned all lands within thofe precincts mentioned by the Order dated 21ft day of July, 1739, Excepting Nich. Davies; Reafon is unknown to us. Colo. Benjamin Harrifon's line is unknown to us.

ALEX'R MOSS, JOHN HARWOOD,
JAMES POWELL COCKE,
Copy Teft. JAMES COCKE.

All the Gentlemen are agreed in our purfinks without proceffioning.

CHARLES WOODSON, JOHN WILLIAMSON,
JAS HATCHER,
JAMES POWELL COCKE,
Copy Teft. JAMES COCKE.

AT A VESTRY held at the Court Houfe, for Henrico parifh, the 5th day of May, 1740, prefent—James powell Cocke, James Cocke, Church Wardens; Richard Randolph, John Redford, Bowler Cocke, John Povall, Wm. Fuller and John Williamfon, Gent., Veftrymen.

Peter Randolph, Gent., who was formerly chofen to be Veftryman of this parifh, now comes and takes the Oaths appointed and is thereupon Admitted accordingly. Prefent—Peter Randolph, Gent.

The Clerk Informs the Veftry that the Several perfons, who were appointed proceffioners for the year 1739, have made returns of their proceedings, which, by him, is regiftered in the parifh Book; whereupon the Church Wardens do proceed to Examine and Atteft the Same.

The Veftry do fell the Twenty five Thoufand pounds of Tobacco levy'd in October laft, for the ufe of the parifh, unto Colo. Richard Randolph, who agrees to give for the fame after the rate of Ten Shillings per hundred, Current money. It is thereupon Ordered that the Collector do pay him the Said Tobacco as Soon as he can Conveniently Collect the Same.

AT A VESTRY held for Henrico parifh, the 13 Day of October, Anno Dom. 1740: prefent—Mr. William Stith, Clerk; James po'l Cocke, James Cocke, Gent., Church Wardens; Richard Randolph, John Redford, Bowler Cocke, John Williamfon and Wm. Fuller, Gent., Veftrymen.

Henrico Parifh, Dr., for the year 1740.

	Neet Tob'o.
To the Rev'd Mr. William Stith, One Sallary,	16,000
To 4 per ct. on do. for Cafk,	640
To fo much towards building the New Church,	20,000
To Sackville Brewer, Reader at Curl's Church,	1,789

To do. as Clerk of the Veftry,	430
To do. as late Collector for Infolvents, &c.,	1,069
To John Eals, Reador at Chappel,	1,789
To John Hopfon, Sexton at Curl's Church,	536
To Elenor Williams, Do. at Chappel,	536
To the Church Wardens, for Communion Bread and Wine,	344
To John North, for keeping Mary Burnett,	896
To Edmond Allen, for keeping his Son, an Idiot,	536
To Robert Hardwick, for keeping his Son,	430
To the Church Wardens, for the ufe Elizabeth Baley,	600
To Do. for Rebecca pruit,	600
To Do. for John Weft, an Infant,	400
To Do. for Jane Jennings,	715
To Do. for Benjamin Good, a Blind man,	800
To James po'l Cocke, for a Scrubbing brufh for ye Church,	20
To the Church Wardens, for Elenor Green,	200
To fo much to be fold for money to pay James Hatcher his Ballance for Building a Barn on the Glebe,	2,000
	50,330
To Commiffion on 53,486@6 per ct is	3,209
	53,539

Per Contra Credit:

By 1,138 Tythables, @ 47 ℔s. per pole, is	53,486
By Ball'e due to the Collector,	53
	53,539

Mr. William Fuller is appointed parifh Collector for the Enfuing year, and it is ordered that he do receive of every Tithable perfon within the parifh, forty Seven pounds of Tobacco, and if any perfon refufe to pay the fame, he is to Deftrain for it; he enters into Bond for the performance thereof. John Redford and John Williamfon, Gent., are his Securities.

Richard Randolph, Gentleman, produces a letter Directed to him, from the Hon'ble William Byrd, Efquire, which is read as followeth, Viz:

"October 12, 1740.

"SIR:

"I fhould, with great pleafure, oblige the Veftry, and particularly your felf, in granting them an Acre to build their Church upon, but there are fo many roads already through that Land, that the Damage to me would be too great to have another of a mile long cut thro' it. I fhould be very glad if you would pleafe to think Richmond a proper place, and confidering the great number of people that live below it, and would pay their Devotions there, that would not care to go fo much higher, I can't but think it would be agreeable to moft of the people, and if they will agree to have it there, I will give them two of the beft lots, that are not taken up, and befides give them any Pine Timber they can find on that Side Shockoe Creek, and Wood for burning of Bricks into the bargain. I hope the Gent. of the Veftry will believe me a Friend to the Church when I make them the Offer, and that I am both theirs,

"Sir, and

"Your moft Humble Serv't,

"W. BYRD."

Whereupon the queftion is put whether the faid Church fhould be Built on the Hill caled Indian Town, at Richmond, or at Thomas Williamfon's plantation on the Brook Road, and is carryed by a majority of voices for the former. It is thereupon Ordered that the Church, formerly Agreed to be Built by Richard Randolph, Gent., on the South Side of Bacon's Branch, be Built on Indian Town, at Richmond, after the Same manner as in the faid Former Agreement, was mentioned.

JAMES P'L COCKE,
JAMES COCKE.

AT A VESTRY, held at the Court House, for Henrico parifh, ye 6 day of July, 1741: Prefent—Richard Randolph, James p'l Cocke, Bowler Cocke, John Povall, William Fuller, James Cocke and John Williamfon, Gent., Veftrymen.

It is ordered that Mr. William Fuller, the parifh Collector, do Sell what Tobacco he now hath in his hands, belonging to the parifh, this day at publick Sale for Cafh, to the higheft bidder, and that he fell the remainder of the faid parifh Tobacco, which he hath not yet Collected, in Like manner, at Aug'ft Court next.

JAMES P'L COCKE,
JAMES COCKE,
} *Church Wardens.*

AT A VESTRY held for Henrico Parifh, the Seventh day of Decem'r, 1741: prefent—The Rev'd Mr. William Stith, James Po'l Cocke and James Cock, Gent., Church Warden; Richard Randolph, John Bolling, Bowler Cocke, John Redford, John Povall, William Fuller and Peter Randolph, Gt., Veftrymen.

Dr. Henrico Parifh, for the year 1741.

To the Rev'd Mr. William Stith, his Sallery and Cafk,	16,640
To Sach. Brewer, Reador,	1,789
To Do. as Clerk of the Veftry,	450
To Do. for Infolvents in Anno 1741,	212
To John Eals, Reador,	1,789
To John Hopfon, Sexton,	636
To the Church Wardens, for Benja. Goode, blind,	800
To Do. for Rebecca pruet,	600
To Do. for Elenor Green,	250
To Do. for Communion Bread and Wine,	344
To Mary North, for keeping Mary Burnet,	896
To Edmond Allen, for his Son, an Idiot,	536
To the Son of Robert Hardwick, Lame,	430
To Ball'e due to Mr. Fuller, late Collector,	53
To Do. for Infolvents, &c.,	752
To Wm. Porter, Jun'r, over charged Anno 1740,	53
	26,666
To Com. on 28,224 @ 6 per ct,	1,693
	28,359

Henrico parifh is Cr. for the year 1741.

By 1,176 Tithables at 24 per pole is	28,224
By Ballance due to the Collector,	135
	28,359

Richard Royal, Gent., is appointed Collector of the parifh Levy for the Enfuing year, and it is ordered that he do receive of Every tithable perfon in the faid parifh, the fum of twenty-four pounds of tobacco, and in cafe of a refufal or delay he is to deftrain for the fame.

Beverly Randolph, Gent., enters himfelf Security.

Mr. William Fuller prefents an Acct of the tobacco fold by him as Collector, for the ufe of the Parifh, which is ordered to be lodged with the Clerk.

JAMES P'L COCKE,
JAMES COCKE.

AT A VESTRY held for Henrico parifh, October ye 2d, 1742: Prefent—The Rev'd Mr. William Stith, Min'r; James Powell Cocke and James Cocke, Church Wardens; Richard Randolph, John Bolling, Bowler Cocke, John Povall and Robert Mofby, Veftrymen.

Dr. Henrico Parifh for the year 1742.

	N't Tob'o.
To the Rev. Mr. William Stith, his Sallery and Cafk,	16,640
To John Eals, a Reador at Upper Church,	1,789
To John Hopfon, Sexton at Curl's Church,	536
To the Church Wardens, for Communion Bread and Wine,	344
To Richard Royal, Collector for a Bal. for laft year due to him,	135
To the Church Wardens, for the ufe of Benjamin Good, Blind,	1,200
To Do. for Rebeccah Pruit,	600
To Do. for Elenor Green,	250
To Mary Hughs, for keeping Mary Burnet,	896
To Edmond Allen, for keeping his Son,	536

To Church Wardens, for Elizabeth Hamlet,	800
To Do. for Edward Skinner,	600
To James Powel Cock, for his Advance for Benjamin Good and Elizabeth Hamlet, Cafk, £3. 11. 6. in Tob'o,	600
To Sack. Brewer, for fifteen months Sallary as Reador, and Cafk Included,	2,236
To Do. for Clerk of the Veftry, Cafk included,	447
To Do. for Surveying the Glebe,	430
To Mary Bennet, for keeping Wm. Weft, a poor Orphant,	800
To Church Wardens, for Jane Jennings,	1,000
To Do. for Elizabeth Baley,	600
To fo much towards Building a Chapel at Deep Run,	10,000
To John Hutchen, for the Church Wardens to difpofe of for his Ufe,	406
	41,381
Com's for Collector,	2,488
	43,869

Do. Parifh is Cr.

By Richard Royal, Collector for Tob'o Rec'd of perfons not Seffed,	504
By 1,239 Tithables at 35 Tob'o per pole is	43,365
	43,869

Richard Royal, Gent., is appointed Parifh Collector for the enfuing year, who enters into bond Accordingly. John Bolling and John Povall, Gent., enters themfelves securities.

On the petition of Thomas Fenton and others, it is agreed and ordered that a Chappel be built on the hill above Deep Run on the main road, on the land of*
to be in length, forty Eight; and Breadth, Twenty four—to be weatherboarded with Fetheredge planck and covered with hart shingles, nailed on—to have three Pews, Reading Defks,

*Illegible.

Pulpit and Gallery, to be finifhed workmanlike in a plain, ftrong manner.

And it is agreed that the Veftry do meet at Curl's Church on the laft Saturday in November next, To Treat with undertakers about building the said Chappel, of which the Church Wardens are to give Notice.

Beverley Randolph, Gent., is chofen a Veftryman in the room of Mr. Edward Curd, dec'd.

JAMES PO'L COCKE,
JAMES COCKE.

AT A VESTRY held for Henrico Parifh, at Curl's Church, July 16, 1743: Prefent—James Powell Cocke and James Cocke, Church Wardens; Richard Randolph, John Redford, John Povall, Beverly Randolph and John Williamfon, Gentlemen, Veftrymen.

Beverly Randolph, Gent., having been formerly elected a member of this Veftry, in the room of Mr. Edward Curd, deceafed, now comes and takes the Oaths as by law appointed to qualifie him self for that office.

John Coles, Gent.,[17] is chofen a Veftryman in the room of Mr. William Fuller, dec'd. Thomas Mofby and William Finney are chofen in the room of John Bolling & Bowler Cocke, Gent., who are moved out of the Parifh.

Purfuant to an Act of Affembly of this Colony, and in Obedience to an order of Henrico County Court, The Parifh is Divided into several precincts, and perfons appointed in each precinct to go in proceffion and renew the Bounds of each perfons Land.

Firft Precinct:

Ordered that Thomas Hughes, Thomas Ellis and William Ellis, with the Affiftance of their Neighboring freeholders, do fometime before laft day of March next, go in proceffion and renew the bounds of all lands from the mouth of Great Weftham to William Gordon's, thence upwards all between Gordon's Road and James River, to the head of the parifh. And that the faid Thomas Hughs, Thomas Ellis and Wm. Ellis, or any two of them, do take and return to this Parifh Veftry an Account of every perfon's land by them proceffioned, Together with the Names of thofe prefent, an alfo what lands they fhall fail to proceffion, and the particular Reafon of fuch failure.

Second Precinct:

From William Gordon's Road to the head of the Parifh; thence to Chickahominy Swamp, and down that to Turner's Run, and up Hungry Branch to the head of Afnam Brook and from thence to Gorden's aforesaid. Ifaac Winftone, Jofeph Parfons and William Britain, appointed proceffioners.

Third Precinct:

All between Chickahominy Swamp and Afnan Brook to the head of faid Brook. Ludwell Bacon, Matthew Hopfon and William Owen, Appointed proceffioners.

Fourth Precinct:

All between Chickahominy Swamp and the Brook Road, as low as Cannon's and Smith's Mill. Robert Sharp, John Pleafant and Silvanus Walker, are appointed proceffioners.

Fifth Precinct:

All between the mouth of Gilley's Creek and Great Weftham Road, on the River, and to extend back as far as Cannon's and Gorden's. Jofeph Hopkins, John Langford and Robert Sharp, Jun'r, are appointed proceffioners.

Sixth Precinct:

From the mouth of Gilley's Creek, on James River, to William Lewifes, on Chickahominy Swamp, Thence upwards as high as Cannon's and Smith's Mill. Nathaniel Vanderwall and John Gunn, and Edward Curd, are appointed proceffioners.

Seventh Precinct:

All between Gilley's Creek and Coneliuf's, from the River, back as far as the Seven Pines Road, and as low as the Southern Branch Bridge. William Finney, John Giles and Nicholas Giles, are appointed proceffioners.

Eighth Precinct:

All between Corneliuf's and Two mile Creek, the main County road and the river. Edward Cox, John Stewart and Benj. Burton appointed proceffioners.

Ninth Precinct:

All between Two mile Creek, Four Mile Creek, James river and the main Country road. Jofeph Woodfon, Henry Sharp and Francis Pierce, proceffioners.

Tenth Precinct:

All between Corneliuf's and Four mile Creek, from the main Country Road, to Seven Pines Road. William Whitlow, Darby Enroughty & Charles Caffy, proceffioners.

Eleventh Precinct:

All between William Lewif's and Boar Swamp, on Chickahominy, to Extend back as the Head of Boar Swamp. Richard Williamfon, Julius Allen and Andrew Matthews, appointed proceffioners.

Twelf Precinct:

From the mouth of Boar Swamp to the County line on Chickahominy Swamp, thence to Extend Southward as far as the fork of Long Bridge Road. John Cocke, John Hale and Thomas Binford, proceffioners.

Thirteenth Precinct:

All between Four Mile Creek, Bailey's Run and White Oak Swamp, the beft. Robert pleafant, Mathias Ayrs and Pew. Price, appointed proceffioners.

Fourteenth Precinct:

All between Bailey's Run, the County Line and the Weftern Run. Charles Woodfon, James Hatcher and John Williamfon, proceffioners.

Fifteenth Precinct:

All between the head of Bailey's Run, the Weftern Run and the County line, to extend Northward as far as the fork of the long bridg Road. William Porter, Jun'r, John Middleton and Stephen Woodfon, proceffioners.

JAMES P'L COCKE,
JAMES COCKE,
C'h Wardens.

AT A VESTRY, held at Curl's Church, for Henrico Parifh, on Fryday, xvj day of December, Anno q. Dom. 1743: John Coles, Gent., who was formerly elected a member of this Veftry in the room of Mr. William Fuller, deceafed, now comes and takes the Oath of a Veftryman, and is thereupon admitted, as ufual.

Prefent.

Richard Randolph, Beverley Randolph, John Redford, John Povall, James powell Cocke, John Williamfon and John Coles, Gent., Veftrymen.

Dr. Henrico Parifh for the year 1743.

	Net Tob'o.
To the Rever'd Mr. William Stith, his fallery and cafk,	16,640
To John Eals, Reador, fallery and cafk,	1,789
To Mark Clark, Reador, fallery and do.	1,789
To Sack. Brewer, Clerk of Veftry, proceffioning year,	895
To John Hopfon, Sexton at Curl's Church,	536
To Elenor Williams, Do. at Chapel,	536
To the Church Wardens, for Communion Bread and Wine,	344
To the Church Wardens, for the ufe of Benj. Good, blind,	1,500
To Mary Hughes, for keeping Mary Burnet,	896
To Edmond Allen, for keeping his fon, an Idiot,	1,000
To the Church Wardens, for Elizabeth Hamlet,	800
To Do. for the ufe of Ann Skinner, a poor widow,	400
To the Church Wardens, for Jane Jennings,	1,000
To do. for Elizabeth Bailey,	600
To Martha Bennett, for keeping orph't Will Weft till Ap'l Next,	400
To the Church Wardens, for Rebeccah Pruit,	600
To Colo. Richard Randolph, for ufe of John Hutchens,	400
To Thomas Pirkins, for keeping Ann Evans a Year,	300
To Colo. Richard Randolph, for ufe of William Ford,	600
To Do. for lame phelemon Childers,	500
To John Forfic, for keeping Nehemiah Watfon three months,	250

To Cock, for £1. 19. 9, Advanced for faid Watfon,	230
To the Church Wardens, for the ufe of Nehemiah Watfon,	1,200
To John Hopfon, for clearing ye Church Yard formerly,	100
To William Street, for Reading Prayers at Deep Run,	1,000
	34,405
To Comm'on on 34,405 ℔s. Tob'o, at 6 per ct., is	2,064
	36,469
Ballance due from ye Collector to the Parifh,	641
	37,110

Henrico Parifh is Cred'r.

By 1,237 Tithables, at 30 per pole, Affeffed, 37,110

James Cock, Gent., is appointed Collector, who gives Bond Accordingly; Richard Randolph and Beverley Randolph, Gent., his Securitys.

Beverly Randolph and John Coles, Gent., are chofen Church Wardens for the Enfuing year, who take the Oath Accordingly.

Beverley Randolph, Gent., agrees to Build on the Gleebe a Tobacco Houfe, Forty feet Long and twenty broad, to be well framed with good Timber, and covered with good Shingles, Nailed on; to be finifhed in every refpect Workmanlike, according to the manner of Such fort of Houfes, for which he is to receive Twenty pounds Curr't Money.

BEVERLEY RANDOLPH,
JOHN COLES, } *Ch. Wardens.*

Henrico Parifh, in Obedience to the Worfhipful Gentlemen of the Veftry, we, the Subfcribers, have proceffioned all the Lands in our precinct; only part of a line between Steven Floyd's and Steven Woodfon's not agreed, and Wm. Griffin refufes to proceffion. Mr. John Pleafants neglected to proceffion his land.

WM. PORTER, Jun'r,
JOHN MIDDLETON.

Copy Teft.

A return of' the order of the Veftry for proceffioning the Bounds alloted to Robert pleafant, Matthew Ayres and Pew Price, lines not proceffioned, as Follows: Edward Good, Ju'r, he not being willing; Tho. Matthew, Edward Good, line Trees not to be found; Colo. Richard Randolph's lines being newly done; Robert Pleafants, Edward Good, Jr., line trees not to be found; Thomas Pleafants, James Woodfin, refufing to go; John Hobfon, Eliza Hobfon, bounds not made between them.

Copy Teft.

Purfuant to an order of Veftry, we have given notice to all the Free holders in our precinct, and have accordingly gon in proceffion on all the Lines of thofe who would attend us.

CHARLES WOODSON,
JAS. HATCHER,
JOHN WILLIAMS.

Copy Teft.

By a Veftry held at Curl's Church, Dated July 16, 1743, we have proceffioned thefe Lines: The line of William and Francis Pierce and Robert Blairs, Abraham Childers, there with us; the line of William Sharp and Robert Blaufe,, Ifack Sharp and Abraham Childers with us; then the line of John Redford and John Bolling, John Redford and Abraham Childers with us; then the line of John Bolling and Hays Whitlow, Hays Whitlow, Junior, in the Room of his Father, and John Redford, Abram Childers with us; then the lines of Robert Cott, Negro Jane and Hays Whitlow, Negro Jane, Henry Whitlow, Negro Jane, John Frazure, Negro Jane, Hays Whitlow, Abraham Childers, John Red there; then the line of William Stone and John Frazure, Philemon Pirkins, John Frazure there; then the line of William Stone and John Frayfer, Philemon Perkings, Wm. Stone, John Frayfure there; then the lines of John Redford, Senior, and Robert Blaufe, Robert Blaufe not there, John Redford there and Abraham Childers there; then the lines of Abraham Childers and Francis Redford, his Father, John Redford, in his room, and Abraham Childers with us; then the line of Philemon Perkins and John Frayzur, John Frafure, John Redford, Abram Childers there; then the line of Jofeph Woodfon and

Philemon Pirkins and Robert Blaus, Abraham Childers, John Redford there with us; then the line of Jofeph Woodfon and Robert Blaufe, John Redford, Abraham Childers there; then the line of Jofeph Woodfon and Abraham Childers, John Redford, Sen'r, Abraham Childers there; then the line of John Redford, Sen'r, and Abraham Childers, they there; then the line of John Redford, Jun'r, and Fran's Redford, by order of their Father; then the line of John Redford and Milnor Redford, by order of their Father; all thefe lines being peacably proceffioned by us.

JOSEPH WOODSON,
HENRY SHARP,
FRAN'S PIERCE.

Copy Teft. Feb'y 22, 1743.

In Obedience to an Order of Henrico Court, we, the Subfcribers, have gon in proceffion and renewed the Bounds of the Several Tracts of Land within the limits of the faid Order, in the prefence and with the Confent of the proprietors of the faid lands, as Witnefs our hands and c this 3rd day of ffeb., 174¾.

ROBERT SHARP,
Copy Teft. JOHN PLEASANTS, Jr.

All the Patented Land in our precincts, according to the direction of the order, all perfons being prefent by us.

DARBY INRUFTY,
Copy Teft. CHARLES CASSY,
WILLIAM WHITLOW.

Whereas, by order perfent Lands, John Pheris, Thomas Elmore, William Gathrit, one line don joining Elmore; Capt. James Cocke not done; proceffioned Jofeph Childers, Charles Winfrey, Anthony Matthews, Edward Allen, Arobria Elmor, Martin Martin, Jofeph Watfon, Richard Williamfon, William Ives, William Sprague, John Leafon, Edward Dean, Julius Allen, Thomas Bethel, John Warner, Ephraim Gathrit, Richard Truman, Thos. Spragin, all quietly proceffioned By Richard Williamfon, Julius Allen, Antho. Matthews.

Copy Teft.

John Cocke, Thomas Binford, John Hales: We have proceffioned all the Lands to be found in our Bounds.

Copy Teft. March 20, 1744.

AT A VESTRY held at Curls Church, For Henrico Parifh, the 19th day of November, 1744: Prefent—the Rev-er'd William Stith, Minifter; Beverley Randolph and John Coles, Church Wardens; Rich'd Randolph, James Powell Cocke, John Redford, Peter Randolph and John Povall, Veftrymen.

Dr. Henrico Parifh for ye year 1744.

	Net Tob'o.
To. Mr. William Stith, Sallery and Cafk,	16,640
To John Eals, Reador,	1,789
To Mark Clark, Reador,	1,789
To Sack Brown, Clerk of the Veftry,	450
To Bowler Cocke, for Recording Deed of Church Land,	86
To John Hobfon, Sexton,	536
To Elenor Williams, Do.,	536
To Church Wardens, for Bread and Wine,	344
To Do., for the ufe of Benjamin Good,	1,500
To Thomas Hughes, for keeping Mary Burnet,	896
To Edmond Allen, for his Son, an Idiot,	1,000
To Church Wardens, for Elizabeth Hamlet,	500
To Do., for Ann Skinner,	400
To Mr. Burnert, for keeping Will Weft, laft year,	400
To Church Wardens, for Jane Jennings,	1,000
To Do., for Elizabeth Bailey,	600
To Do., for Rebecca Pruit,	600
To Colo. Richard Randolph, for John Hutchens,	400
To Do., for William Ford,	600
To Do., for Lame Childers,	500
To Henry Cox, for Ann Evans,	400
To the Church Wardens, for Nehemiah Watfon,	800
To William Street, Reador at Deep Run,	1,789
To Samuel Gathrit, for keeping William Daniel,	700
To Church Wardens, for Clothes for faid Daniel,	200
To Jofeph Hopfon, for keeping his Lame son,	800

To the Church Wardens to be fold for the ufe of the Parifh,	10,000
	45,255
To Commiffion, at 6 per ct,	2,715
	47,970
Ball'e due to the Parifh,	223
	48,193

Parifh Cr. for the year 1744.

By James Cocke, laft year Collector, for a Ball'e in laft Levy, and Tob'o rec'd of Perfons not lifted, according to his own Acc't,	1,213
By 1,305 Tithables, at 36 per pole,	46,890
	48,193

James Cocke, Gent., is appointed Parifh Collector for the enfuing year, who gives Bond accordingly. Richard Randolph and Peter Randolph, Gent., enter themfelves fecuriteys.

Peter Randolph and John Coles, Gent., are appointed to agree with the cheapeft workmen they can, to undertake and Finifh the Chappel to be Built at Deep Run, and to report their proceedings in the premifes to the next veftry.

Beverley Randolph, Gent., is Impowered and defired by the Veftry to fend to England, as foon as conveniently he can, for the Following things, on the Parifh account, viz: One Parfon's Surplis, a Pulpit Cufhion and Cloth, Two Cloths for Reading Defks, a Communion Table Cloth, and a Dozen of Cufhions to be of good Purple Cloth, and the Surples good Holland; alfo a large Bible and four large Prayer Books.

BEVERLEY RANDOLPH,
JOHN COLES, Signed.

AT A VESTRY, held at the Court Houfe, for Henrico Parifh, the 2d day of December, 1745: Prefent—the rev'd

Mr. William Stith, Minifter; Beverley Randolph and John Coles, Church Wardens, Richard Randolph, Peter Randolph, James Cocke, William Finney and John Redford, Gent., Veftrymen.

Dr. Henrico Parifh for the year 1745.

	Nett Tob'o.
To the Rev. Mr. William Stith, Minis'r, Sallery and Cafk,	16,640
To John Eals, Reador,	1,789
To Mark Clark, Reader,	1,789
To William Street, Reader,	1,789
To Richard Deane, Clerk of the Veftry,	450
To John Hopfon, Sexton,	536
To Eleanor Williams, do.,	536
To the Church Wardens, for Bread and Wine,	344
To do., for the ufe of Benjamin Goode,	1,500
To do., for keeping Mary Burnet,	896
To Edmond Allen, for his fon, an Idiot,	1,000
To the Church Wardens, for Elizabeth Hamlet,	500
To do., for Jane Jennings,	1,000
To do., for Elizabeth Baley,	600
To do., for Rebecca Pruit,	600
To Colo. Richard Randolph, for William Ford,	600
To do., for Lame Childers,	500
To the Church Wardens, for Nehemiah Watfon,	800
To Jofeph Hobfon, for keeping his lame son,	800
To John Coles, Church Warden, for the Ballance of £6. 3. 9½d, w'ch is now due to him as p'r his acco't, and if it overpays the faid Ball., he is to account for it in the next Levy,	1,000
To the Church Wardens, for Jane Jennitt,	1,200
To John Shoemaker, for clearing the arbor at Deep Runn, and for an Acre of Land to fet the Chappel upon,	536
To James Hatcher, for making a coffin for John Hutchens,	80
To William Lawlefs, for keeping Mary Burnet's baftard child—the faid Mary Burnet being an Idiot and upon the Parifh,	700

To Abraham Baley, for burying Mary Gwinn, a mulatto, a poor p'fon, who happened to be taken ill and dyed at his Houfe,	100
To the Church Wardens, to be fold for the ufe of the Parifh,	11,215
	47,500
To Commiffion on 7,500, at 6 per cent.,	2,850
	50,350
To Samuel Gathrite, to be paid out of ye above Ball'ce, w'ch was ord'd to be fold,	400
Ballance due from the Collector,	400
	51,150

Do. Parifh Cr. for the year 1745.

By 1,325 Tithables, at 38 per pole,	50,350
By Hobfon's Allowance difallowed,	800
	51,150

Ordered—

That William Gay, Collector, receive of each Tithable in the Parifh thirty Eight pounds of Tobacco per poll, who gives Bond according. Peter Randolph & John Archer, Gent., his Securities.

Ordered—

That Richard Deane is appointed Clerk of the Veftry.

Ordered—

That the Ballance due from the Collector, being Nine pounds & Eight pence be paid to Colo. Richard Randolph.

Ordered—

That the Ballance in Mr. Redford's hands, for Colo. Bolling's tiths, three pounds four fhillings, be paid likewife to Colo. Richard Randolph.

BEVERLEY RANDOLPH,
JOHN COLES, Signed.

AT A VESTRY, held at Varina, for Henrico Parifh, December 2, 1746:

Present.

The Rev. William Stith, Richard Randolph, Peter Randolph, John Coles, William Finney, John Redford & John Povall, Gent., Veftrymen.

Henrico Parifh for the year 1746.	
To the Rev'd William Stith, Minifter, fallery and cafk,	16,640
To John Eals, reader,	1,789
To Mark Clark, reader,	1,789
To William Street, reader,	1,789
To Richard Deane, Clerk of the Veftry,	450
To John Hobfon, Sexton,	536
To Elenor Williams, do.,	536
To John Shoemaker, for keeping and cleaning the arbor,	536
To the Church Wardens, for Bread and Wine,	344
To Colo. Richard Randolph, for the ufe of Ben. Goode	1,500
To the Church Wardens, for Jane Jennings,	1,000
To do., for keeping Mary Burnet,	896
To do., for keeping Elizabeth Baley,	600
To do., for Rebecca Pruit,	600
To Edmond Allen, for his Son, and Idiot,	1,000
To Colo. Richard Randolph, for William Ford,	600
To do., for Lame Childers,	500
To the Church Wardens, for James Jennit,	1,200
To William Lawlefs, for keeping Mary Burnet's baftard Child—fhe being an Idiot and upon the parifh,	700
To Thomas Wood, for gates & and fencing, &c., to the Upper Church yard,	2,000
To Eleanor Williams, for making curtains, &c., for the Upper Church,	300
To Nicholas Giles, for one Levy overlifted in 1744,	36
To Charles Floyd, for one Levy laft year overcharged,	36
	35,377
To Commiffions on 35,377 at 6 per ct,	2,123

To Richard Deane, for 12 Infolvents at 36 each,	432
To Ballance to be paid to the Church Wardens, to be fold for ye ufe of ye P'rifh,	6,706
	44,638

Henrico Parifh, Cr.

By Major John Coles, his Tob'o, ball'e as per acc't,		1,102
By do., Cafh Acco.	6. 17. 12	
By a Ball'ce due from Rich'd Royal, w'ch the Ch. Wardens are defired to receive,	4. 1. 8	
By a Ball'ce due from Colo. Richard Randolph, as per Acco. 51. 19. 10,		504
By 1,304 Tithes, at 33 per polle,		43,032
		44,638

Ordered—

That Richard Randolph & John Coles, Gent., be appointed Church Wardens for the enfuing year.

Ordered—

That Richard Deane be appointed Parifh Collector, and that he receive of every Tithable thirty three pounds of Tobacco, in cafe of refufal, to disftrain for the fame, and to give Bond and Security to the Church Wardens accordingly.

RICHARD RANDOLPH,
JOHN COLES,
Signed.

AT A VESTRY, held at Curl's Church, for Henrico Parifh, August 4th, Anno 1747, for dividing the Parifh into feveral precincts, and appoint perfons to go in proceffion and renew the bounds of Land according to law.

Prefent.

The Rev'd Mr. Will'm Stith, Minifter; Rich'd Randolph, John Coles, Church Wardens; Peter Randolph, John Redford, James Powel Cocke, John Poval, John Williamfon, Rob't Mofby, Veftrymen.

First Precinct.

Purfuant to an Act of Affembly of this colony, and in obedience to an Order of Henrico Court, it is ordered that Henry Ellis, Charles Ellis, John Ellis and William Harding, w'th the Affiftance of their neighboring free holders, do sometime before the laft day of March next, go in proceffion and renew the Bounds of all lands from the mouth of Weft Ham to Will'm Gordon's, thence upwards and between Gordon's Road and James River to the head of the parifh; and that the faid Henry Ellis, Charles Ellis, Mr. John Ellis, Will'm Harding, (or any two of them,) do take and return to this Parifh Veftry an Account of Every perfons I and by them proceffioned, together with the names of thofe prefent, and alfo what Land he fhall fail to proceffion and the particular reafon of fuch failure.

Second Precinct.

From the mouth of Meredith's Branch to the head of it, and from thence to the head of Eaftern Branch, thence down the faid Branch to Gordon's Road, including all the land Between the Eaftern Gordon's Road, Hanover and Goochland lines. Peter Purryear, Rich'd Lovatt, Richard Eaft and Edward Pryor, are appointed Proceff'rs.

Third Precinct.

From the mouth of Turner's Run to the head, thence to the mouth of hungry, thence to the head of the faid Run, and from thence to the head of the Brook, including all the lands to the Brook, and in the Fork thereof and Gordon's road, and fo up to the Eaftern Branch, thence up that Branch to the head of Meredith's, down the Chickahominy Swamp, down the Swamp to the place began at. Rich'd Holland, Rob't Webb, John Shepard & Thomas Bowles, Jun'r, are appointed Proceff'rs.

Fourth Precinct.

All between Chickahominy Swamp and Upland Brook to the head of the faid. Langstone Bacon, Wm. Pattman, Stephen Panky and Thomas Owen, are appointed Proceff'rs.

Fifth Precinct.

All between Chickahominy Swamp and the Brook road, as

low as Mary Cannon's and Smith's Mill. Jos. Pleafants, Jun'r, John Smith, Obadiah Smith, John Britain, pro'rs.

Sixth Precinct.

All between the mouth of Gilley's Creek and Weft Ham, on the river, and to extend back as far as Gordon's and Mary Cannon's. Rob't Cooke, Wm. Sneed, Jno. Price, Jacob Smith, are appointed proceffioners.

Seventh Precinct.

From the mouth of Gilley's Creek, on James River, to Jos. Lewif's, on Chickahominy Swamp, thence upward as high as Smith's Mill and Mary Cannon's. Jof'h Lewis, Ed. Curd, Daniel Price, ——fon Daniel, William Smith, are appointed proceff'rs.

Eighth Precinct.

All between the mouth of Gilley's creek and Corneliuf's, on James river, and to extend back as far as Seven Pines road, and as low as the Southern Branch Bridge. Matthew Herbert, Jno. Alday, Sen'r, George Roberfon and Brazure Cock, are appointed proceff's.

Ninth Precinct.

All between Corneliuf's and Two mile creek, on the River, and to extend back as far as the Main Country Road. John Cox, John Bullington, Wm. Parker, Thos. Perkins, are appointed proceff'rs.

Tenth Precinct.

All between Two mile Creek, Four mile Creek, James river, and the main Country road. Ifaac Sharpe, John Frazure, Wm. Pierce and Haife Whitlo, app'd proceff'rs.

Eleventh Precinct.

All between Corneliuf's and Four mile Creek, on the main road, thence as far back as the Seven pines road, Including the Fork of Boar Swamp. Thomas Bethel, Fran's Wagftaff, Richard Truman and John Weft, appointed proceffioners.

Twelfth Precinct.

All between Lewif's, Boar Swamp, Chickahominy Swamp, and the Seven pines road. William Gathright, Thos. Ellmore, Edmund Allen, Wm. Ferrifs, Sen., appointed proceffioners.

Thirteenth Precinct.

From the mouth of Boar Swamp, on Chickahominy, to the lower bounds of the parifh line fouthward as far as where the road forks for Long Bridge and Bottom Bridge. Rich'd Moore, Jno. Carter's fon, Gerrard Ellyfon and Sam'l Bugg, Sen'r, app'd proceffioners.

Fourteenth Precinct.

From Bailey's Run to Four mile Creek; all between the road that leads from Four mile creek bridge to Chickah'y Swamp and James river, Including the fork of White Oak Swamp. Samuel Gathright, Thomas Matthews, John Childers and Edward Goode, are appointed proceffioners.

Fifteenth Precinct.

All between Bailey's Run and the lower bounds of the Parifh, to extend back as far the Weftern Run, John Pleafant's, Bailey's. Nich's Hobfon, Wm. Hobfon and John Pleafants, at Curle's, appointed proceff'rs.

Sixteenth Precinct.

All between the Weftern Run, the head of Bailey's Run and the Parifh line, to extend northward as far as the fork of Long bridge road. John Middleton, Humphrey Smith, Stephen Woodfon and Robert Mattox, appointed proceffioners.
Ordered—

That Solomon Carey be appointed Clerk of the Veftry in the room of Richard Deane, deceafed, and that John Bryant be appointed a clerk in the room of John Eales, who is become incapable of executing his office. His fallary to commence from the first day of June last.

RICHARD RANDOLPH,
JOHN COLES, Signed.

AT A VESTRY, held at Colo. Richard Randolph's, for Henrico Parish, January 19th, 174$\frac{7}{8}$.

Prefent.

The Rev'd William Stith, Richard Randolph, Church Wardens: Peter Randolph, John Povall, John Redford, Jno. Williamfon and Robert Mofeby, Veftrymen.

Dr. Henrico Parifh for the year 1747.

To the Rev'd William Stith, S'lary & cafk,	16,640
To John Eals, for reading 7 months at the Up'r Chu'h,	1,039
To John Bryant, for 5 months as ditto,	750
To Mark Clark, read'r,	1,789
To William Street, reader,	1,789
To Solomon Cary, Clerk Veftry, proceffioning y'r,	895
To John Hobfon, fexton,	536
To Elenor Williams, do.,	536
To John Shoemaker, for keep'g and clean'g the arbor,	536
To the Church Wardens, for Bread and Wine,	344
To Colo. Richard Randolph, for the ufe of Benja. Goode,	1,500
To the Church Wardens, for Jane Jennings,	600
To do., for keeping Mary Burnet,	896
To do., for Eliza. Bailey,	600
To Edmond Allen, for his fon, an Idiot,	1,000
To Colo. Richard Randolph, for William Ford,	600
To do., for Lame Childers,	500
To do., for James Jennitt,	600
To William Lawlefs, for keeping Mary Burnett's baftard child, fhe being an Idiot, on the Parifh,	600
To the Church Wardens, for Rebecca Pruit,	600
To Daniel Baker,	600
To John Liptoott,	600
To Anna Smith,	400
To Edward Goode, for curing George Macon's hand,	489
To Charles Ballou, for Infolvents,	200

To the Church Wardens, to be fold for the ufe of the pa'h,	8,989
To Commiffions on 46,410, at 6 per ct,	2,784
	46,410

Henrico Parifh, Cr.

By 1,326 Tithes, at 35 per poll,	46,410

Richard Randolph, Jun'r,[18] William Randolph,[19] Daniel Price & William Lewifs, are elected veftrymen in the room of John Coles & Powell Cocke, deceafed, and James Cocke & Will'm Finney, who have removed out of the Parifh.

Richard Randolph, Jun'r, takes the oath by the law prefcribed, and is admitted to his place in the Veftry.

Peter Randolph, Gent., is chofen Church Warden.

Ordered that the house upon the Gleeb be repair'd, & an addition of 20 feet at each end, with two windows in each room, and that the Church Wardens be impowered to agree with workmen; and the Chimneys to be pull'd down & rebuilt.

Ordered that the Church Wardens do pay to Andrew Barclay £7. 13. 3¼, due to him from the Veftry, & do receive of Maj'r Coles' Eftate £3. 0. 6, the Ball'nce due to the Veftry.

Ordered—

That Francis Redford and Charles Ballou be appointed parifh Collector, and that they receive of every tith thirty five pounds of tobacco—in cafe of refufal, to diftrain for the fame—who gives bond and Security accord'ly.

RICHARD RANDOLPH,
PETER RANDOLPH,
Church Wardens.

AT A VESTRY, held at Chatfworth, for Henrico Parifh, January 24th, 1748-9.

Prefent.

The Reverend William Stith, Peter Randolph, Church Warden; John Poval, Thomas Mofely, William Randolph, Robt. Mofeby, Jno. Williamfon and Jno. Redford, Gent., Veftrymen.

William Lewis having taken the Oath of a Veftryman takes his feat accordingly.

Dr. Henrico Parifh for the year 1748.

To the Reverend William Stith, Minifter, Salary and cafk,	16,640
To John Bryant, reader,	1,789
To Mark Clarke, do.,	1,789
To William Street, do.,	1,789
To Solomon Cary, Clerk Veftry,	450
To John Hobfon, Sexton,	536
To Elenor Williams, do.,	536
To John Shoemaker, for Cleaning the Arbour,	536
To the Church Wardens, for Bread and Wine,	344
To do., for keeping Mary Burnett,	1,000
To the Church Wardens, for Jane Jennings,	600
To Colo. Richard Randolph, for the ufe of Benja. Goode,	896
To the Church Wardens, for Elizabeth Bailey,	850
To Edmond Allen, for his fon, an Idiot,	1,000
To Colo. Richard Randolph, for Wm. Ford,	600
To do., for Lame Childers,	500
To the Church Wardens, for James Jennett,	800
To William Lawlefs, for keeping Mary Burnet's baftard child, fhe being an Idiot, and upon ye Parifh,	600
To Robert Morris, for burying Rebecca Pruitt,	200
To Daniel Baker,	600
To John Liptrott,	400
To Anne Smith,	300
To Peter Randolph, for keeping Eliz'a Bailey the remaining part of her life,	600
To John Jones, for keeping his Daughter, being a Fool,	300
To Humphrey Smith, for keep'g Thomas Bethel,	500

To Godfrey Piles, for a levy overcharged in 1746,	33
To Charles Ballow, for infolvents,	490
To the Church Wardens, to be fold for the ufe of the Parifh,	16,349
To Commiffion on 54,284 ℔ Tob'o at 6 p. ct.,	3,257

Henrico Parifh Cr.

By 1,324 Tithables at 41 per poll,	54,284

Ordered—

That the Church Wardens take the neceffary method to recover 6,706 pounds Tob'o, Levied in 1746, for the ufe of the parifh, w'ch was collected by Richard Deane, and not Accounted for.

John Poval and Peter Randolph, Gent., are appointed Church Wardens for the enfuing year, and have taken the Oath Accord'ly.

Ordered—

That the Church Wardens Agree with Workmen to build a houfe upon the Gleebe, 48 by 20, two outfide chimneys, a cellar 20 by 20, to be finifhed Strong, Neat and Plain.

Jno. Ellis is Elected Veftryman in the room of Daniel Price, who refufes to act.

JOHN POVALL,
PETER RANDOLPH,
Church Wardens.

We, the fubscribers, in Obedience to an order of the Veftry, held at Curl's, for Henrico Parifh, have proceffioned the lands within the precincts hereafternamed, viz.: between Corneliuf's and four mile Creek, thence back to the feven pines Road, Including the fork of Boar Swamp; the line between Garrard, Robert Ellyfon and Richard Trueman, Not proceffioned on the Acco't of the faid Richard Trueman; And the line between William Burton (living in Goochland) and Benj. Burton, not proceffioned, the faid William not prefent. Frans Wagftaff, Jno. Weft, Richard Truman, Junr., Thomas Bethell; 25th March, 1748.

Copy Teft.

Purfuant to an order of Henrico Court, we, the fubfcribers, have proceffioned all the following lands: Capt. Jno. Walton's land, Capt. John Williamfon's land, Henry Stoke's land, Nathaniel Bacon's land, William Bacon's land, Ifaac Winfton's land, William Owen's land, John Owen's land, Matthew Hobfon's land, Jno. Law's land, Eliza Watkin's land, John Orange's land, Jno. Cornet's land, William Ford's land, John Mofeby's land, James Brittain's land, James Jones' land, Thos. Conoway's land, David Terey's land, Ro. Sharp's land, William Hillery's land, James Crawford's land, Daniel Fitz Patrick's land, John Bois' land, and all other lands to us directed. Given under our hands this 24th day of March, 1747-8.

WILLIAM PALMER,
LANGSTONE BACON,
STEPHEN PANKY,
Copy Teft. THOMAS OWEN.

Purfuant to an order of Veftry, we, the Subfcribers, have made a quiet and peacable proceffion of all the lands within our precincts, except Colo. Benjamin Harrifon, who did not appear.

JOHN MIDDLETON,
HUMPHREY SMITH,
Copy Teft. ROBERT MATTOX.

All the lands proceffioned in Precincts, excepting Thomas Watkins, and the reafon is he will not fhow his line. Mary Cannon's is Orfands Land. Colo. Benja. Harrifon no attendance, Gilligrew Marin, no attendance.

JOSEPH LEWIS,
EDW'D CURD,
DANIEL PRICE,
Copy Teft. WILLIAM SMITH.

In obedience to an order of Henrico Court, We, and each of us, hath gone in and proceffioned and renewed the bounds of all lands between the Mouth of Gilley's Creek and the Weft Ham on the river, and hath Extended back as far as

Gordon's and Mary Cannon's, with a peacable and quiet proceffion from under our hands.

ROBERT COOKE,
JOHN PRICE,
JACOB SMITH,
WILLIAM SNEED.

Copy Teft.

We, the Subfcribers, have proceffioned all the lands within our proceffion, according to the order of Veftry, only Michael Gathright, it being not bounded.

EDMOND ALLEN,
THOMAS ELMORE,
WILLIAM GATHRIGHT,
WILLIAM FERRIS.

Copy Teft.

In Obedience to an Order of Veftry, to us directed, we have, with the affiftance of the Neighbors and Freeholders in our Precinct, proceffioned all the lands therein, Save the lines Annexed, viz.: A line between John Pleafants, senr., and Chas. Woodfon, the line not plain and no line.

A line between John Pleafants, Senr., and Bowler Cocke, the line not plain and the faid Bowler Cocke not prefent, Hindered.

A line between John Pleafants, Senr. and John Pleafants Jr., no line.

A line between do. and Thomas Holmes, no line.

Three lines between James Hatcher and do., no lines.

A line between Jno. Pleafants, Junr., and do., no line.

A line between Jno. Pleafants, Junr. and Charles Woodfon, no line.

A do between do., and Bowler Cocke, the Same Reafon.

The line between Bowler Cocke and Thomas Holmes, no line.

The line between James Hatcher and Bowler Cocke, no line.

The line between Richard Randolph and Bowler Cocke, not done, by reafon neither party would attend.

The line between Richard Randolph and Jas. Pleafants, not done, by reafon of Randolph's not attending.

Richard Randolph, of Curls,
Builder of the Original Church.

The line between James Cocke and John Poval, not done, Cocke not attending.

The line between Charles Carter and Peter Burton, not done, Carter being an infant.

John Povall's and Chas. Floyd's line joining Chas. Carter, not done by the fame reafon.

John Povall's lines between him and Robert Poval, not done, Robert being an infant.

Signed by the Proceffioners.

JOHN PLEASANTS, JUNR.,
NICHOLAS HOBSON,
JOHN PLEASANTS, (Curles,)
Copy Teft. WILLIAM HOBSON.

AT A VESTRY held at Richmond the 16th day of Nov., 1749.

Prefent.

The Reverend William Stith, Thomas Mofeby, John Redford, Wm. Lewis, Rob't Mofeby, John Williamfon, John Povall and William Randolph.

Rich'd Rocket is chofen Clerk of the Veftry in the room of Solomon Cary.

Bowler Cocke elected a Veftryman in the Room of Richard Randolph, Efqr., Died; William Randolph, Efqr., Elected Church Warden in the room of Peter Randolph, Efqr., and took the oaths accordingly.

JOHN POVALL,
WILLIAM RANDOLPH.

AT A VESTRY held at Varina February 6th, 1749-50.

Prefent.

The Reverend William Stith, William Randolph, Church Warden; Thomas Mofeby John Renford, William Lewis, John Ellis, Bowler Cocke, Gent.; Vestryman, John Williamfon.

Henrico parifh is Dr. for ye year 1750.

To William Stith, Minifter, Salary and Cafk,	16,640
To John Bryan, reader,	1,789

To Mark Clarke, Ditto,	1,789
To William Street, Ditto,	1,789
To Richard Rocket, Clerk of the Veftry,	536
To John Hobfon, Sexton,	536
To Elenor Williams, do.,	536
To the Church Wardens, for Bread and Wine,	344
To John Shoemaker, for cleaning of Chapple,	536

STITH.

AT A VESTRY, held at Richmond Town, the 8 Day of February, 1750.

Prefent.

The Rev'd William Stith, Minifter, William Randolph and John Povall, Church Wardens.

Peter Randolph, Thomas Mofeby and William Lewis, Gentlemen Veftrymen.

Bowler Cocke, John Ellis, Gent'm, take the Oaths to the Government and Subfcribe the Teft, an accordingly admitted.

Henrico Parifh Dr. for the year 1750.

To William Stith, Minifter, S'lary & cafk,	16,640
To John Bryan, reader,	1,789
To Mark Clark, do.,	1,789
To William Street. Ditto,	1,789
To Richard Rocket, clk. of the Veftry,	450
To John Hobfon, fexton,	536
To Elenor Williams, do.,	536
To the Church Wardens, for Bread and Wine,	344
To John Shoemaker, clean'g the chapple,	536
To Benjamin Goode,	1,500
To the Church Wardens, for Jane Jennings,	600
To do., for keeping Mary Burnet,	896
To Edmond Allen, for his fon, an Idiot,	1,000
To the Church Wardens, for William Ford,	600
To do., for Lame Childers,	500
To do., for James Jinnitt,	800
To do., Daniel Baker,	600
To John Jones, for keeping his daughter, a Fool,	300

To William Lawlefs, for keeping Mary Burnett's child from the firft of Auguft till this time,	300
To Robert Mofeby,	180
To the Church Wardens, for Francis Archer,	300
To Do., for the Widow Hanfford,	500
To lie in the Church Warden's hand till further orders,	13,156
To Commiffion 6 per ct.,	2,739
	47,880

Cr.

By 1,368 Tithables, at 35 per pole, 47,880

WILLIAM RANDOLPH,
JOHN POVALL,
Ch. Wardens.

AT A VESTRY, held at Richmond Town, the 29 day of September, 1750.

Prefent.

The Reverend William Stith, Minister, William Randolph and John Povall, Church Wardens.

John Redford, Bowler Cocke, John Ellis and John Williamfon, Gent'n Veftrymen.

Henrico Parifh Dr. for the year 1761.

To William Stith, Minifter, fallery and cafk,	16,640
To John Bryan, Reader,	1,789
To Mark Clarke, Do.,	1,789
To William Street, Do.,	1,789
To Richard Rocket, Clerk of the Veftry,	450
To John Hobfon. Sexton,	536
To Elenor Williams, Do.,	536
To John Shoemaker, Do.,	536
To the Church Wardens, for Bread and Wine,	344
To Benjamin Goode,	1,000
To Jane Jennings,	600
To Mary Burnett,	890
To Mary Allen, for her Son, an Idiott,	1,000

To William Ford,	600
To Limme Childers,	500
To James Jennitt,	800
To Daniel Baker,	600
To Francis Archer,	300
To the Widow Hanfford,	500
To John Oakling, for keeping James Brown 6 weeks and burying him,	200
To John Burton, for Sundry Goods brought for Mary Brown, and Carrying her to Blifland Parifh,	300
To Johnathan Williams, for repairing the Church Yard, &c.,	50
The Church Wardens, to be paid John Shoemaker, when he acknowledges a deed for one Acre of Land whereon the Deep Run Church ftands,	100
To Doctor Hopper, for cutting off Cowfell's Arms,	500
To lie in the Church Warden's hands till further orders,	14,807
	47,162
To Commiffion at 6 per ct.,	2,818
Cr.	49,980
By 1,470 Tithables, at 34 per poll,	49,980

JOHN POVALL,
WILLIAM RANDOLPH.

AT A VESTRY, held at Richmond Town, August ye 17, 1751.

Prefent.

The Reverend Mr. William Stith, Minifter; William Randolph and John Povall, Church Wardens; Richard Randolph, John Redford, John Ellis, John Winston and Robert Mofeby, Veftrymen.

Purfuant to an Act of Affembly of this colony, and in obedience to an Order of Henrico Court, the Parifh is divided into Precincts, and perfons appointed in each precinct to Proceffion and renew the Bounds of each perfons Land.

Firft Precinct.

Ordered—

That Richard Cottrel, John Lancafter, Jofeph Ellis and Jofeph Freeman, with the Affiftance of the Neighbouring freeholders, do, before the laft day of March next, proceffion and renew the bounds of all lands from the Mouth of great Weftham to William Gordon's, thence upwards between Gordon's Road and James River to the head of the Parifh; and that the faid Richard Cottrell, John Lancafter, Jofeph Ellis and Jofeph Freeman, or any two of them, do take and return to the Veftry an Acco. of every Perfons Land by them Proceffioned, together with the names of thofe prefent, and alfo what land they fail to proceffion, and the Particular reafon of such failure.

2nd.

From William Gordon's Road to the head of the Parifh, thence to Chickahominy Swamp, and down that to Turner's Run, and up Hungry Branch to the head of land Brook, and from thence to Gordon's Aforefaid. Robert Mofeby, Junr., Theopilus Favours, Richard Holland, Wm. Brittain, are appointed Proceffioners.

Third Precinct.

All between Chickahominy Swamp and Ofland Brook to the head of the faid Brook. Henry Stokes, William Bacon and Jofeph Parfons, Junr.

4th.

All between Chickahominy Swamp and the Brook Road, as low as Cannon's and Smith's Mill. John Pleafants, John Smith and Drury Wood.

5.

All between the Mouth of Gilley's Creek and great Weftham on the River, and to extend as far back as Cannon's and Gordon's. William Deriguid, Dacy Southall and John Gunn.

6.

From the Mouth of Gilley's Creek on James River to Jno. Lewis on Chickahominy Swamp, thence upwards as high as Cannon's and Smith's Mill. Thomas Watkins, William Price and Thomas Cocke.

7.

All between Gilley's Creek and Corneliuf's, from the River back as far as the Seven Pines Road, and as low as the Southern Branch Bridge. David Burton, John Alday, Jr., Thomas Alday and Nicholas Giles, Junr.

8.

All between Corneliuf's and Two Mile Creek, James River and the Main Country Road. Milner Redford, Hays Whitlow, Lufby Turpin and Thomas Jordan.

9.

All between two Mile Creek,, Four Mile Creek, James River, and the Main Country Road. William Sharpe, William Pierce and Francis Pierce.

10.

All between Corneliuf's and Four Mile Creek, from the Main County Road to Seven Pines Road. John Whitlow, James Whitlow, William Whitlow and Richard Reynard.

11.

All between William Lewif's and Boar Swamp on Chickahominy, to extend back as far as the head of Boar Swamp. Julius Allen, Martin Martin and Anthony Matthews.

Twelfth Precinct.

From the Mouth of Boar Swamp to the County Line on Chickahominy, thence to extend Southward as far as the Long Bridge Road. George Pyke, Thomas Watkins and John Hales.

13.

All between Four Mile Creek, Bailey's Run and White Oak Swamp. Jos. Hobfon, Jno. Hobfon and Saml. Gathright.

14.

All between Bailey's Run, The County Line and the Weftern Run. Charles Woodfon, James Hatcher and Step. Wood.

15.

All between the head of Bailey's Run, the Weftern Run and the county line, to extend Northward as far as the fork of the Long Bridge Road. John Middleton, Humphrey Smith and Edward Eaft.

Ifaac Winfton, Junr., is Elected a Veftryman in the room of Beverly Randolph, Efqr., deceaf'd.

WILLIAM RANDOLPH,
JOHN POVALL.

AT A VESTRY, held at Richmond Town the 3d day of December, 1751.

Prefent.

The Reverend Mr. William Stith, Minifter; William Randolph and John Povall, Church Wardens; Richard Randolph, Bowler Cocke, Junr., William Lewis, John Williamfon, Robert Mofeby and John Ellis, Gent., Veftrymen.

Richard Randolph, John Williamfon, Gent'm, are elected Church Wardens in the room of Wm. Randolph and John Povall, and took the Oath Accordingly.

Ordered—The Churchwardens do agree with the workmen to repair and Paint the Church at Curle's, and do whats neceffary to the Church at Richmond.

Henrico Parifh Dr., for the year 1752.

To William Stith, Minifter,	17,280
To John Bryan, Reader,	1,789
To Mark Clarke, Do.,	1,789
To William Street, Do.,	1,789
To Richard Rockett, clk. Veft'y ye proceffi'g year,	895
To John Hobfon, Sexton,	536
To Ellenor Williams, Do.,	536
To John Shoemaker, Do.,	536
To the Church Wardens, for Bread and Wine,	344
To Benjamin Goode,	500
To Mary Burnett,	896
To Mary Allen, for her fon, an Idiott,	1,000
To William Ford,	600
To Lemme Childers,	500
To Daniel Baker,	600
To Francis Archer,	400

To Thomas Bates, for keeping Ann Smith laft year,	300
To Ann Smith, for the enfuing year,	300
To John Liptrott,	400
To lie in the Church Warden's hands till further orders,	14,962
To Obadiah Robinfon,	500
To Commiffion at 6 per cent,	2,784
	49,236
Cr.	
By 1,492 Tythables @ 33 per pole,	49,236

The Reverend Mr. William Stith refigns this Parifh the firft day of October next, he being chofen Minifter of S. Anns; and it is ordered that the Church Wardens write to the Reverend Mr. Rofcow Cole, to make him an offer of the Parifh.

Mark Clarke is difmifed from the office as Clerk of Curl's Church.

RICHARD RANDOLPH,
JOHN WILLIAMSON.

In Obedience to the Within order, we, the Subfcribers, have gone in proceffion and renewed the bounds of the feveral tracts of land within the limits to us prefcribed, in the prefence of and the confent of the proprietors of the faid lands, all excepting a line between Capt. John Williamfon and Cuthbert Williamfon, an orphan, which we were forbid to do. Witnefs our hands this 21 Feb'y, 1752.

JOHN PLEASANTS,
JOHN SMITH,
DRURY WOOD.

Copy Teft.

AT A VESTRY, held at Richmond, the 22d day June, 1752.

Prefent.

The Hon'ble Peter Randolph, Efqr., Mr. William Stith, Minifter; Richard Randolph and John Williamfon, Church Wardens; Bowler Cocke, Junr., William Randolph, John Ellis and William Lewis, Gentlemen, Veftrymen.

The Reverend Mr. Jofeph Bewfher is unanimously elected

Minifter in the room of Mr. William Stith, to enter on his office the firft day of October next. Mark Clark is elected Clerk of Curl's Church in the room of his father.

JOHN WM'SON,
RICHARD RANDOLPH.

AT A VESTRY, held in Richmond Town the 25th day of Auguft, 1752.

Prefent.

The Hon'ble Peter Randolph, Efqr., Richard Randolph and John Williamfon, Church Wardens; John Povall, Bowler Cocke, William Lewis and John Ellis, Gentlemen, Veftrymen.

Mr. Samuel Duval[20] is elected a Veftryman in the Room of John Redford, Deceafed.

Mr. Jofeph Lewis is Elected a Veftryman in the room of Ifaac Winfton, who refufeth to act.

The Reverend Mr. Miles Selden[21] is unanimously elected Minifter in the room of Mr. Jofeph Bewfher, who refigns this Parifh, to enter on his office the firft day October next.

RICHARD RANDOLPH.
JOHN WM'SON.

AT A VESTRY, held at Richmond Town the 8th day of December, 1752.

Prefent.

The Rev'd Miles Selden, William Randolph, John Williamfon, John Povall, Bowler Cocke, Jr., William Lewis, John Ellis and Robt. Mofeby, Gent. Abraham Conley, Jr., is chofen clark of the Veftry in the room of Rich'd Rockett, who having refigned.

Samuel Du Vall and Jofeph Lewis, Gent., take the Oaths to the Government and Subfcribe the Teft. Ordered—That the Minifter perform Divine Service at the Upper Church once in five Weeks. Ordered—That Mr. Samuel Du Vall value the Porches of the Gleabe, and that the Church Wardens pay Colo. Bland what they fhall be valued at over and above his agreement. Ordered—That the Church Wardens agree with workmen to raile the Church yard and to pail in a garden at the Gleabe.

Ordered—That the Collector allow Sarah Scott 500 ℔ of Tobo. out of the fines due to this Parifh, and that Wm. Green be allowed five hundred pounds of Tobo. out of the fines. Judith Ruff, exempted from paying the Parifh Levy.

Bowler Cocke, Jr., and Samuel Du Vall, Gent., are appointed Church Wardens for the enfuing year.

Henrico Parifh,	*Dr.*
To the Rev'd Mr. William Stith, for one half year's Sallery,	8,320
To the Rev'd Mr. Miles Selden,	8,320
To John Bryant,	1,789
To Mark Clark, Jr.,	1,789
To William Street,	1,789
To Richard Rockett, late clk. Veftry,	500
To John Hobfon Sexton,	536
To Elenor Williams, Do.,	536
To John Shoemaker, Do.,	536
To the Church Wardens, for Bread and Wine,	344
To Benjamin Goode,	500
To Mary Burnet,	896
To Mary Allen, for her Son, an Idiot,	1,000
To William Ford,	600
To Lemmy Childers,	500
To Daniel Bacon,	600
To Francis Archer,	400
To Ann Smith,	300
To John Liptrott,	500
To Obadiah Robinfon,	400
To Margaret Leigh, for taking care of Lucy Freeman,	300
To lye in the hands of the Church Wardens till further orders,	11,205
To the Collectors Commiffions,	2,730
	45,510

Cr.

By 1,517 Tithables at 30 ℔ Tobacco per pole,	45,510

BOWLER COCKE, SAML. DU VAL.

AT A VESTRY, held at Richmond Town the 15th day of October, 1753.

Prefent.

The Rev'd Miles Selden, William Randolph, Bowler Cocke, Richard Randolph, Robert Mofeby, John Williamfon, Jofeph Lewis, John Ellis, Samuel Du Vall and William Lewis, Gent. Veftry.

Henrico Parifh,	*Dr.*
To the Rev'd Miles Selden,	16,640
To John Bryan, clk.,	1,789
To Mark Clark, Junr.,	1,789
To William Street,	1,789
To Abraham Cowley, clk. Veftry,	500
To Thomas Holmes, fexton,	536
To Elenor Williams,	536
To John Shoemaker,	536
To the Church Wardens, for Bread and Wine,	344
To Benjamin Goode,	500
To Mary Burnett,	896
To Mary Allen, for her Son, an Idiot,	1,000
To William Ford,	600
To Lemmy Childers,	500
To Danniel Baker,	400
To Francis Archer,	500
To Anne Smith,	500
To John Liptrott,	500
To Margaret Leepor, for taking care of John Lee,	500
To James Lucas,	200
To Matthew Bridgeman, for taking care of Obadiah Robinfon,	232
To the Rev'd Miles Selden, fhort levy'd laft year,	665
To the Rev'd Miles Selden, four per ct. on his Sallery, allowed by him,	300
To Benjamin Goode, for keeping Freeman's child,	500
To John Goode and his Wife,	333
To Lye in the hands of the Church Wardens till farther orders,	20,139
	53,424

To the Sheriff's Commiffions,	3,197
Cr.	56,651
By 1,490 Tithables, at 30 ℔ Tob'o per pole,	56,621

Nathaniel Bridgewater is exempted from paying the Parifh Levy.

Ordered—That the Church Wardens pay the William Stith twenty-four pounds ten fhilling for the work done to the Gleabe at Varina.

Ordered—That the Church Wardens pay to John Williamfon sixteen pounds eleaven and fix pence for money expended on the Poore of the Parifh.

Ordered—That the Church Wardens Agree with Workmen to Build a Hen Houfe, and Repair and move the ftable on the Glebe.

William Randolph and Jofeph Lewis are appointed Church Wardens for the enfuing year.

Ordered—That Richard Randolph pay the money in his hands to the Church Wardens.

WILLIAM RANDOLPH,
JOSEPH LEWIS.

AT A VESTRY, held at Richmond Town, Nov. 7th, 1754.

Prefent.

The Rev'd Miles Selden, William Randolph, Jofeph Lewis, John Williamfon, John Povall, William Lewis, John Williamfon and Samuel Du Vall, Gent. of the Veftry.

Henrico Parifh,	*Dr.*
To the Rev'd Miles Selden,	17,150
To John Bryan, clk.,	1,789
To Mark Clarke, Junr.,	1,789
To William Street,	1,789
To Abraham Cowley, Clerk Veftry,	500
To Thomas Hoomes, Sexton,	536
To Elenor Williams,	536
To John Shoemaker,	536
To the Church Wardens, for Bread and Wine,	344
To Benjamin Goode,	500

To Mary Burnet,	896
To Mary Allen, her fon, an Idiot,	1,000
To William Ford,	600
To Lemmy Childers,	500
To John Liptrott,	500
To Francis Archer,	400
To Margaret Lee, for taking care of John Lee,	500
To James Lucas,	500
To Benjamin Goode, for taking Freeman's child,	300
To John Goode and his wife,	500
To Robert Yaxley, for keeping Elinor Addam's Child,	500
To lye in the hands of the Church Wardens till further orders,	1,425
	33,090
To the Collector's Commiffions,	1,985
	35,075
Cr.	
By 1,525 Tithables, at 23 per pole,	35,075

John Povall and Jofeph Lewis are chofen Church Wardens for the enfuing year.

Ordered—That the Prefent Church Wardens pay the ballance of twenty feven pounds feaventeen fhillings and two pence, which they have in their hands, to the Church Wardens for the Enfuing year.

Ordered—That the Church Wardens pay Samuel Du Vall feaven pounds feven fhillings and fix pence, the Ballance of his acco't for repairing the Church at Curls.

JOHN POVALL,
JOSEPH LEWIS.

AT A VESTRY, held at Richmond Town, July 25th, 1755.

Prefent.

William Randolph, William Lewis, John Povall, Bowler Cocke, John Ellifs, Samuel Du Vall, John Wiliamfon, Jofeph Lewis.

Purfuant to an Act of Affembly of this Colony and in obedience to an order of Henrico Court, the Parifh, as divided into precincts, and perfons appointed in each precinct to proceffion and renew the bounds of each perfons land.

Firft Precinct.

Ordered—That Richard Cottrell, David Staples, Henry Ellifs, and Jofeph Ellifs, with the affiftance of the Neighboring Freeholders, do, before the 11th day of April next, preceffion and renew the bounds of all the lands from the mouth of great Weftham to William Gordon's, thence upwards between Gordon's road and James River, to the head of the Parifh; and that the faid Richard Cottrell, David Staples, Henry Ellifs, William and Jofeph Ellifs, or any two of them, do make and return to this Veftry, an acco't of Every perfon's land by them proceffioned, together with the names of thofe prefent, and alfo what lands they fail to proceffion, and the particular reafon of such failure.

2.

From William Gordon's road to the head of the Parifh, thence to Chickahominy Swamp, and down that to Turner's Run, and up Hungry Branch, to the head of Ofland Brook, and down thence to Gordon's aforefaid. Robert Mofeby, Jr., Jofeph Parfon, Junr., Ifaac Winfton, Jofeph Parfon, Junr. Out.

3.

All between Chickahominy Swamp and Upland Brook, to the head of faid Brook. Nathaniel Bacon, Henry Stokes, Elifha Miller and William Bacon. Out.

4.

All between Chickahominy Swamp and the Brook Road, as low as Cannon and Smith's Mill. John Smith, John Pleafants, Robt. Sharpe, Jr. Drury Wood.

5.

All between the mouth of Gilley's Creek and great Weftham on the river, and to be extended back as far as Cannon's and Gordon's. Jacob Smith, John Gunn, Davy Southall, Valentine Ball.

6.

From the mouth of Gilley's Creek, on James river, to Jofeph Lewis on Chickahominy Swamp, thence upwards as high as Cannon's and Smith's Mill. William Smith, Edward Curd, John Harwood, Nat Vandevall.

7.

All between Gilley's Creek and Cornellyfes, from the river, back as far as Seven Pines Road, and as low as the Southern Branch Bridge. Thomas Aldy, Nicholafs Giles, Junr., Matthew Herbert, Nicholas Malor. Out.

8.

All between Corneliffus and two mile creek, the main county road and the river. John Stewart, Benja. Burton, John Burton, richard renalds.

9.

All between two mile creek, four mile creek, James river and the main co'y road. Milenor Redford, John redford, Francis Pierce and William Parker.

10.

All between Cornellyffes and four mile creek, from the main co'y road to Seaven Pines road. James Whitlow, William Whitlow, Henry Whitlow and Richard Whitlow.

11.

All between Jofeph Lewis and Boar Swamp on Chickahominay, to extend back as far as the head of Boar Swamp. Julius Allen, Anthony Matthews, William Gathwrite and Robert Spears.

12.

From the mouth of Boar Swamp to the co'y line on Chickahominy, thence to extend Southward as far as the Long Bridge Road. Thomas Watkins, Benja. Jordan, John Carter, John White.

13.

All between four mile Creek, Bailey's Run and White Oak Swamp. Jofeph Hopfin, Samuel Gathwrite, William Hopfin, James Linfey.

14.

All between Bailey's Run, the Co'y Line and the Weftern Run Branch. Charles Woodfon, Stephen Woodfon, John Pleafants Bailey, and Robert Pleafants, Junr.

Fifteenth Precinct.

All between the head of Bailey's run, the Weftern Run, and the County Line, to extend Northward as far as the fork of the Long Bridge road. John Martin, Humphrey Smith, John Royfter and John Brackett.

JOHN POVALL,
JOSEPH LEWIS.

AT A VESTRY, held in Richmond Town the 4th day of Nov'r, 1755.

Prefent.

The Rev'd Miles Selden, William Randolph, John Povall, Richard Randolph, Jofeph Lewis, Jno. Williamfon, William Lewis, Samuel Du Vall and rob't Mofeby, Gent., Veftry.

Henrico Parifh,	*Dr.*
To the Rev'd Miles Selden,	17,150
To John Bryan, clk.,	1,789
To Mark Clark, Junr.,	1,789
To William Street,	1,789
To Abraham Cowley,	700
To Thomas Homes, Sexton,	536
To Elenor Williams,	536
To John Shoemaker,	536
To the Church Wardens, for Bread and Wine,	344
To Benjamin Goode,	300
To Mary Burnet,	896
To Mary Allen, her fon, an Idiot,	800
To William Ford,	500
To Lemmy Childers,	250
To John Liptrott	250
To Francis Archer,	300
To Margaret Lee, for the care of John Lee,	400
To Benjamin Good, for the care of Freeman's child,	300

To John Good and wife,	500
To Sufanna Morton,	250
To Matthew Herbert for keeping Freeman's child,	300
To James Woodfin, for keeping Wm. Taylor's children,	400
	30,615
To the Collector's Commiffions,	1,871
To lye in the hands of the Church Wardens,	500
Cr.	33,066
By 1,503, Tythables @ 22 per pole,	33,066

Ordered—That the Church Wardens, repay robert Goode, for 16 Tythables, at 23 per pole, over lifted laft year; likewife repay James Brittain for one Tythe a 23, over lifted laft year.

Richard Randolph and Jofeph Lewis, are elected Church Wardens for the enfuing year.

RICHARD RANDOLPH,
JOSEPH LEWIS.

In Obedience to an Order of Henrico Veftry, we have Proceffion the Lines According to the Within Order, from the mouth of Gilley's Creek to Cannon's, and from thence to Weftham, with Peacable and Quiet Poffeffion. Given under our hands this 7th day of April, 1756.

DASEY SOUTHALL,
JACOB SMITH.

According to the Within Order, we have proceffioned all the lands in our precincts, befides the lines between Capt. James Cock and Thomas Watkins, ye f'd Watkins refufing; and a line between John Williamfon, Junr., and Thomas Franklin, for want of Attendance Apr. 9th, 1756.

WILLIAM SMITH,
NAT VANDERVALL,
JNO. HARWOOD,
EWD CURD.

In obedience to an order of the Veftry, we have procef-

fioned and renewed the bounds of every perfon's lands mentioned in the within order. THOMAS WATKINS,
JOHN CARTER,
ISAAC WHITE.

Purfuant to an order of the Veftry of Henrico, we have, in Obedience to the f'd order, renewed all the lands in our precincts, except as follows: The lands bound between Jofeph Bailey and Hickifon Cox, by reafon of the f'd Cox not being prefent.

The lands between John Cox and Dickinfon Cox, for the reafon aforefaid.

The lands between George Cox, Orphan; Edw'd Cox, Dec'd, and Thomas Perkins; no perfon appearing for f'd Orphan.

The lands between Lifby Turpin and Dickinfon Cox, the f'd Cox not appearing.

The lands between Edw'd Osburn and the aforef'd George Cox, for the reafon aforefaid.

The lands between Thomas Jordan and the f'd George Cox, for the reafon aforefaid.

The lands between Thomas Randolph, orphan of William Randolph, dec'd; and the lands of Jno. Bowling, the Glebe land, Harwood Bullington, William Parker, Thomas Jordan, Robert Bullington; no perfon appearing for the f'd Orphan.

The lands between Jno. Bowling and the Gleabe lands, the f'd Bowling not appearing.

The lands between Jno. Bowling, and Harwood Bullington, an infant, neither parties being prefent.

The lands between John Bolling and Thomas Jordan, for the reafon aforesaid.

The lands between Harwood Bullington, infant, William Parker, no perfon appearing for f'd infant.

The lands between Wm. Epps and Jno. Stewart, Thos. Branch, Wm. Burton, Alex'r Long, Jno. Bowling, William Randolph, Jno. Cox, Benja. Burton: the f'd Wm. Epps not being prefent. JOHN STEWART,
RICHARD RENARD,
JNO. BURTON.

Purfuant to an order of Veftry, we have poffeffioned and renew the bounds of all the lands within the limits to as mentioned in prefence and with the confent of all the proprietors.

ROBERT SHARPE,
JNO. PLEASANTS,
JNO. SMITH,
DRURY WOOD.

Purfuant to an order of the Veftry, we have renewed the bounds of all the lands therein mentioned, excepting a line between Nicholas Medor and Ben. Burton; the parties not agreeing to have done; and Philip Mayo land, no nerfon appearing.

NAT'L BACON,
HENRY BACON,
ELISHA MILLER.

Purfuant to an order of Veftry, we, the Subfcribers, have poffeffioned and renewed all the lines in our precinct.

JAMES WHITLOW,
WM. WHITLOW,
HENRY WHITLOW,
RICHARD WHITLOW.

Purfuant to an order of Veftry, we have renewed the bounds of all the lands therein mention, except as followeth:

Between John Bowling and Jno. Redford, Jno. Bowlinge and Hays Whitlow, Robert Pleafant and Millenor Redford, Jno. Pleafants, Senr., Jno. Pleafants, Junr., and Millenor Redford; they all failing to attend.

MILLENOR REDFORD,
JNO. REDFORD,
FRANCIS PIERCE,
WILLIAM PARKER.

AT A VESTRY, held at Richmond Town January 3d, 1757.

Prefent.

The Rev'd Miles Selden, William Randolph, Bowler Cocke, William Lewis, John Williamfon, Samuel Du Vall, Richard Randolph, Jofeph Lewis and John Elliff, Gent. Veftry.

Henrico Parifh,	*Dr.*
To the Rev'd Miles Selden,	17,150
To John Bryan, clk.,	1,789
To Mark Clark, Junr.,	1,789
To William Street,	1,789
To Abraham Cowley, Clk. Veftry,	500
To Thomas Homes, fexten,	536
To Elenor Williams,	536
To John Shoemaker,	536
To the Church Wardens,	344
To Benjamin Goode,	500
To Mary Allen, her fon, an Ideot,	800
To William Ford,	500
To Lemmy Childers,	250
To John Liptrott,	250
To Francis Archer,	400
To Margaret Lee, for the Care of John Lee,	400
To Benjamin Goode, for the care of Freeman's child,	300
To John Goode and Wife,	250
To Sufanna Morton,	250
To Matthew Herbert, for the care of Freeman's child,	300
To James Woodfin, for the care of Taylor's children,	500
To Edward Pryor, for the care of his child,	250
To the Church Wardens, for the maintainance of John Liggon's wife and child,	800
To lye in the hands of the Church Wardens,	674
To the Collector's Commiffions,	2,003
Cr.	33,396
By 1,518 Tithables at 22 per pole,	33,396

Richard Randolph and Jofeph Lewis is elected Church Wardens for the enfuing year.

RICHARD RANDOLPH,
JOSEPH LEWIS.

AT A VESTRY, held at Richmond Town, December the 5th, 1757.

Prefent.

The Rev'd Miles Selden, William Randolph, Samuel Du Vall, Jofeph Lewis, John Povall, Richard Randolph, William Lewis, John Elliff, Gent. Veftry.

Thomas Adams[22] is elected a Veftryman in the room of John Williamfon, dec'd.

Henrico Parifh,	*Dr.*
To the Rev'd Miles Selden,	17,150
To John Bryan, clk.,	1,789
To Mark Clark, Junr.,	1,789
To William Street,	1,789
To Abraham Cowley,	500
To Agneff Homes, fexton,	536
To Elenor Williams,	536
To John Shoemaker,	536
To the Church Wardens,	344
To Benjamin Goode,	500
To Mary Allen, her fon, an idiot,	800
To William Ford,	500
To Lemmy Childers,	250
To John Liptrott,	300
To Margaret Lee, for the care of John Lee,	400
To Benjamin Goode, for the care of Freeman's child,	300
To John Goode and wife,	300
To Sarah Morton,	240
To James Woodfin, for the care of Taylor's children,	500
To the Church Wardens, for the care of John Liggan's wife and child,	800
To Matthew Herbert for the care of Freeman's child,	300
To Stephen Childers, for the care of his fon's child,	250
To John Shoemaker, for one acre of land where Deep Run Chapel ftands,	100
	30,019
To lye in the hands of the Church Wardens,	2,259
To the Collector's Commiffions,	2,692

Cr.,	24,870
By 1,585 Tiths. at 22 per pole,	34,870

Richard Randolph and Jofeph Lewis are appointed Church Wardens for the enfuing year.

Mr. Samuel Du Vall, Sheriff, is appointed the Parifh Collector for the enfuing year.

Ordered—That the Church Wardens take bond of him according to law.

RICHARD RANDOLPH,
JOSEPH LEWIS.

AT A VESTRY, held at Richmond Town, Dec. 17th, 1758.

Prefent.

The Rev'd Miles Selden, William Randolph, Bowler Cocke, William Lewis, Thomas Addams, Jofeph Lewis, John Ellifs, and Richard Randolph, Gent.

Richard Randolph and Jofeph Lewis are appointed Church Wardens for the enfuing year.

Henrico Parifh,	*Dr.*
To the Rev'd Miles Selden,	17,150
To John Bryan, clk.,	1,789
To Mark Clark, Junr.,	1,789
To William Street,	1,789
To Abraham Cowley,	500
To Agnefs Homes, Sexton,	536
To Elenor Williams,	536
To John Shoemaker,	536
To the Church Wardens,	344
To Benjamin Goode,	500
To Mary Allen, for her Son, an Ideot,	800
To William Ford,	500
To Lemmy Childers,	500
To John Liptrott,	300
To Margaret Lee, for the ufe of John Lee,	700
To Sufanna Morton,	250
To James Woodfin, for the care of Taylor's Children,	500

To the Church Wardens, for the care of John Liggon's Wife and child,	1,200
To William Ford's Wife,	300
To Mary Walters,	500
To Samuel Liggon, for the care of John Liggon's Child,	250
To John Hobfon, for the care of Rob't Down's children two y'rs paft,	600
To the Sheriff for infolvents,	484
To Robert Cooke, for the care of Sufannah, a Mulatto,	400
	32,753
To the Sheriff's Commiffions,	2,151
To lye in the hands of the Church Wardens,	956
Cr.	35,860
By 1,630 Tiths at 22 per Poles,	35,860

Mr. Samuel Du Vall, Sher'f, is appointed the Parish Collector for the Ensuing Year.

Ordered—That the Church Wardens take Bond of him According to Law.

RICHARD RANDOLPH,
JOSEPH LEWIS.

AT A VESTRY, held for Henrico Parish at Richmond Town, Oct'r, 11th, 1759.

Prefent.

The Rev'd Miles Selden, Richard Randolph, Bowler Cocke, William Lewis, John Ellifs, Samuel Du Vall, and Jofeph Lewis, Gent.

Henrico Parifh,	*Dr.*
To the Rev'd Miles Selden,	17,150
To John Bryan, clk.,	1,789
To Mark Clark, Junr.,	1,789
To William Street,	1,789
To Abraham Cowley,	800
To Agnefs Homes, fexton,	536
To Elenor Williams,	536

To John Shoemaker,	536
To the Church Wardens,	344
To Benjamin Goode,	500
To Mary Allen, her fon an Ideot,	1,000
To William Ford and Wife,	500
To Lemmy Childers,	500
To John Liptrott,	300
To Margaret Lee, for the Care of John Lee,	1,000
To Sufanna Morton,	400
To Elizabeth Dorton, for the care of John Liggon's wife,	1,000
To Mary Walters,	500
To Robert Cook, for the care of Sufannah, a Molatto,	200
To Hays Whitlow, for the care of Mary Prevdo's child, a Baftard,	600
To Elizabeth Lucas,	400
To Thomas Watkins, for his care of William Chapman,	400
To the Collector Commiffions,	2,126
To lye in the hands of the Church Wardens,	753
	35,448
Cr.	
By 1,658 Tiths at 21 per pole,	35,448

Mr. Ryland Randolph[23] is Elected a Veftryman in the room of Thomas Mofby who has refigned.

Ordered—That the Church Wardens Agree with the Workmen to Dig & Brick a Well at the Gleab, & make all such repairs as they shall think Necessary & a Greeable to law.

Mr. Philip Mayo, Shf.' is appointed the Parifh Collector for the Ensuing Year. Ordered—That the Church Wardens take Bond and Security of him according to law.

Ordered—That the prefent Church Wardens settle the Acc'ts of Richard Randolph and Lewis, late Church Wardens.

Col'o Richard Randolph and Samuel Duvall are Chofen Church Wardens for the Enfuing Year.

Purfuant to an Act of Affembly of this Colony, and in obedience to an order of Henrico County Court, the Parish is divided in to Precincts and perfons appointed in each Precinct to proceffion and renew the Bounds of each Perfon's land.

1.

Ordered—That Rich'd Cottrell, David Staples, Henry Ellifs, William Ellifs and Jofeph Ellifs, with the Affiftance of the Neighboring Freeholders, do before the 11th day of April next, proceffion and renew the bounds of all the lands from the mouth of Great Weft Ham to William Gordon's, thence upwards between Gordon's road and James river to the head of this parifh, and that the said Richard Cottrell, David Staples, Henry Ellifs, William Ellifs and Jofeph Ellifs, or any two of them, do make and return to this Veftry an acc't of every perfon's lands by them proceffioned, together with the names of thofe prefent, and alfo what lands they fail to proceffion and the particular reafon of fuch failure.

2d.

From William Gordon's road to the head of the Parish, thence to Chickahominy fwamp, and down that to Turner's run, and up Hungary Branch to the head of Upland Brook, and from thence to Gordon's aforefaid—Thomas Wilkinfon, Nathaniel Wilkinfon, Thomas Owen and William Bacon.

3d.

All between Chickahominy Swamp and Upland Brook to the head of the faid Brook—Henry Stokes, Elifha Miller, William Jones and John Mofeby.

4.

All between Chickahominy Swamp and the Brook road, as low as Cannon & Smith's mill—John Smith, John Pleafants, Robert Williamfon and Drury Wood.

5.

All between the mouth of Gilley's Creek and the great Weftham on the river, and to be extended back as far as Cannon's and Gordon's—Jacob Smith, John Gunn, Turner Southall and Benjamin Clarke.

6.

From the mouth of Gilley's Creek, on James River, to Jofeph Lewif's, on Chickahominy Swamp, thence upwards as high as Cannon's and Smith's Mill—William Smith, Edward Curd, John Harwood and Nath'l Vandevall.

7.

All between Gilley's Creek and Cornelliffes, from the river back as far as the Seven Pines Road, and as low as the Southern Branch Bridge—Jacob Burton, Nicholas Giles, Matthew Herbert and Nicholas Meador.

8.

All between Cornelliffes and two Mile Creek, the main County Road and the River—John Stewart, John Burton, fon of Wm. Jofiah Bullington, and Thomas Jordan, Jun'r.

9.

All between two mile Creek, Four mile Creek and the river and the main County road—Milner Redford, John Redford, Francis Pierce and William Parker.

10.

All between Cornellifes and Four mile Creek, from the main County road to Seven Pines road—James Whitlow, William Whitlow, Henry Whitlow and Richard Whitlow.

11.

All between Jofeph Lewis and Boar Swamp, on Chickahominy, to extend back as far as the head of Boar Swamp—Julius Allen, Anthony Matthews, William Gathright and Robert Spears.

12.

From the mouth of Boar Swamp to the County line on Chickahominy, thence to extend Southward as far as the Long Bridge Road—Thomas Waitkins, Ifaac White, John Carter and John Hayles.

13.

All between Four mile Creek, Bailey's Run and White Oak Swamp—Jofeph Hobfin, Samuel Gathright, William Hobfin and Thomas Childrey.

14.

All between Bailey's Run, the County line and the Weftern

Branch—Charles Woodfon, John Pleafants, Jr., Bailey, Robert Pleafants, Jun'r and John Martin.

15.

All between the Head of Bailey's Run, the Weftern Run and the County line, to extend North Ward as far as the fork of the Long Bridge Road—Humphrey Smith, John Royfster, John Middleton and Martin Martin, Sr.

SAMUEL DU VALL,
RICHARD RANDOLPH.

We have proceffioned the lands between Two mile Creek and Fore mile Creek, the River and main County road; the line between Robert Pleafants and Milner Redford, proceffioned—Jno. Pleafants, Robert Pleafants, John Redford and Milner Redford, prefent; the lines between John Redford and Milner Redford agreed, John and Milner Redford, prefent; the lines between John Pleafants and Francis Pierce, failing to meet; the lines between John Bolling and John Redford, not done, Bolling failing to mete; the lines between Hays Whitlow and John Pleafants, Jun'r, not done, Pleafants failing to meet; the lines between John Frazure and Andrew Redford, not done, Andrew under age; likewife Andrew Redford and Robert Scott, not done, the same reafon; the lines between John Bowling and Hays Whitlow, not done, Bowling failing to meet; the line between Jno. and John Redford, agreed, John and Milner Redford, and John Redford, Jun'r, prefent; the line between John Pleafants and John Sharpe, not done, failing to meet; the line between Robert Pleafants and John Redford, agreed, Robert Pleafants and John and Milner Redford, prefent.

JOHN REDFORD,
MILNER REDFORD,
WILLIAM PARKER,
FRANCIS PIERCE.

In Obedience to an Order of Henrico Vesftry, we have gone and proceffioned the lines which we were appointed to do, from Cannon's up Colo. Byrd's line, betwixt Mr. Duvall's and Mr. Byrd, James Patterfon and Drury Wood, prefent; and betwixt Mr. Bird and Drury Wood; Mr. Patterson only by Drury Wood's orders; and betwixt Mrs. Byrd's and Jacob Smith, prefent, Benjamin Clarke and James Patterson; and betwixt John Pierce and the s'd Byrd, prefent, Philip Watfon, John Price and James Patterson; and between John Price and Jacob Smith, prefent, Jacob Smith and Samuel Price; and between John Price, Price and Thomas Williamfon, prefent, Samuel Price, William Miller; and between Jacob Smith and Thos. Williamfon. prefent, William Miller and Samuel Price; and between Robert Williamfon and Cuthbert Williamfon, prefent, William Bacon and Robert Sharpe; and between Cuthbert Williamfon and Jacob Smith; and between Nathaniel Bridgewater and Thos. Wm'fon, prefent, Nat. Bridgewater and William Snead; between Wm. Snead and Wm. Bridgwater; and between Wm. Sneed and Ben. Clarke; between Wm. Bridgwater and Wm. Simes; between Wm. Simes and Jonathan Bridgwater; between Wm. Kelley and Jonath. Bridgwater; between Wm. Kelley and George Kelley; between George Kelley and Ben. Clarke; between John Clarke and Thos. Lewis; between Thomas Lewis and John Gordon and Val'e Ball; between Valentine Ball and Ben. Clarke; between Benjamin Clark and Philip Watfon; between Philip Watfon and William Simms; between William Byrd and Philip Watfon; between William Byrd and Vallentine Ball, with Peacable and Quiet Proceffion, the parties being all prefent. Given under our hands.

BENJA. CLARK,
JACOB SMITH.

According to an Order of Henrico Veftry, we have proceffioned all the lines wihch we were appointed, from the mouth Gilley's Creek to Great Weftham, with a peacable and quiet proceffion in the prefence of Samuel Duvall, James Patterfon, Thomas Wood, William Wood, Thomas Cardwell, John New and John Wood. Given under our hands this 7th day of April, 1760.

JOHN GUNN,
TURNER SOUTHALL.[24]

In Obedience to an Order of Henrico Veftry, we have Peacably and Quietly proceffioned all the lands between the head of Bailey's run, the Weftern run, and the County line, extending as far as the Fork of Long Bridge road. Given under our hands this 6th day of April, 1760.

JNO. ROYSTER,
MARTIN MARTIN.

Purfuant to an Order of Veftry of Henrico County, we have proceffioned and renewed all the lines within mentioned, except the line between Capt. Jofeph Lewis and William Flem'g Cocke—which Cocke refufing to proceffion.

WILLIAM SMITH,
EDW'D CURD,
JNO. HARWOOD,
NATH'L VANDERVALL.

In Obedience to the within Order, we, the fubfcribers have gone in proceffion and renewed the Bounds of the feveral Tracts of land within the limits, to us fubfcribed, being in the prefents and with the confents of the proprietors of the faid lands. Witnefs our hands.

DRURY WOOD,
ROBT. WM'SON,
JNO. PLEASANTS,
JNO. SMITH.

Purfuant to an Order of Henrico Veftry, directed to us, we, the fubfcribers, have renewed the bounds of every perfons land within the bounds of faid order—Prefent, Rich'd and Robert Moore, Ephraim Gathright, William Bottom, William Ferris, Robert Ferris, John Bottom, George Adams, William Davis, Richard Whitlock, Francis Wilkinfon, Robert Pleafants and Martin Martin, Jun'r, Geoge Clopton and Thomas Bottom. March 27th, 1760.

THOMAS WATKINS,
JOHN CARTER,
ISAAC WHITE.

In Obedience to an Order of the Veftry of Henrico Parifh, we, the fubfcribers having given notice to all the freeholders within our Precinct, have gone with and renewed the lines of the feveral perfons as mentioned below, viz:

Firft, we went on the lines between Charles Woodfon and William Hatcher—the said Hatcher refused to proceffion, saying it was not a line agreeable to his patent; prefent, Richard Randolph and Ryland Randolph. Thence to the line between John Pleafants, his son Robert Pleafants and Richard Randolph, the Mark Trees were, without opofition renewed. Thence on the line between the faid John Pleafants, Jr., and Wm. Hatcher's—the faid Hatcher refufing to proceffion for the fame reafon as between him and Charles Woodfon. Thence on the lines between John Pleafants and John Pleafants the younger—the faid John Pleafants, Jun'r, refufing to proceffion, he alledging that if the line between him and William Hatcher is not right this cannot be fo, feing they muft be parallel; prefent, Richard Randolph, Bowler Cocke, John Pleafants, William Hatcher and all the proceffioners. At the fame time, the faid William Hatcher ordered us to make the proper return, which we acquainted Richard Randolph, one of the Church Wardens, with. Thence on the line between Ryland Randolph and Bowler Cocke quietly proceffioned and the lines renew'd. Thence on the line between the faid Cocke and Richard Randolph done as aforefaid. Thence on the line between the faid Randolph and John Pleafants, Jun'r, done as aforefaid; prefent, Wm. Hatcher, Bowler Cocke and all the Proceffioners. Thence on the line between John Povall's and Robert Povall, done quietly and all the lines renewed. Thence on the line between Charles Floyd and John Povall, done as aforefaid. Thence on the line between the faid John Povall and Stephen Woodfon, done as aforefaid. The other lines between thofe parties being Water Courfes; prefent, John Pleafants, Charles Woodfon, John Martin, John Povall, Charles Floyd, Charles Floyd, Robt. Povall and John Chriftian, Jr. All the other lines within our Precinct were not proceffioned by the parties not attending.

Given under our hands this 11th day of April, 1760.

CHARLES WOODSON,
JOHN PLEASANTS, Jr.,
ROBERT PLEASANTS, Jr.,
JOHN MARTIN.

We have proceffioned all the lands that is within the within mentioned bounds without any objection.

WILLIAM HOBSON,
SAM. GATHRIGHT.

AT A VESTRY, held at Richmond Town, Dec'r 2nd, 1760:

Prefent.

The Rev'd Miles Selden, William Randolph, Richard Randolph, William Lewis, Robert Mofby, Jofeph Lewis, Ryland Randolph, Samuel Duval, John Ellis and Thos. Adams.

Henrico County,	*Dr.*
To the Rev'd Miles Selden,	17,150
To John Bryan, cl'k,	1,789
To Mark Clarke,	1,789
To William Street,	1,789
To Abraham Cowley,	500
To Agnes Homes, sexton,	536
To Elenor Williams, do.,	536
To John Shoemaker,	536
To the Church Wardens,	344
To Benjamin Goode,	500
To Mary Allen, her fon an idiot,	1,000
To William Ford,	500
To Lemmy Childers,	500
To John Liptrott,	500
To Margaret Lee, for the care of Jno. Lee,	1,000
To Sufannah Morton,	500
To Elizabeth Dolton, for the care of John Liggon's wife,	1,000
To Mary Walters,	500
To Thos. Watkins, for the care of Wm. Chapman,	400
To Abrah'm Cowley, for Infolvents,	840
To Richard Allen, for keeping Margaret Childers,	200
To the Church Wardens, for keeping Ursley Green,	500
To Sarah Wotton,	300

To the Collector's Commiffions,	2,246
To Ly in the hands of the Church Wardens,	1,989
	37,444

Cr.

By 1,702 Tiths, at 22 per pole,	37,444

Ordered that the Sheriff Collect twenty-two Pounds of Tob'o Pole for the ufe of the Parifh.

Thomas Mofeley refigns his place in the Veftry, and Ryland Randolph is chofen in his room.

Ryland Randolph and Thos. Adams are chofen Church Wardens for the enfuing year.

THOS. ADAMS,
RY. RANDOLPH.

AT A VESTRY, held at Richmond Town, October 3d, 1761:

Prefent.

The Rev'd Miles Selden, Richard Randolph, Bowler Cocke, William Lewis, John Ellis, Jofeph Lewis, Samuel Duvall, Ryland Randolph and Thomas Adams, Gent.

Henrico Parifh,	*Dr.*
To the Rev'd Miles Selden,	17,150
To John Bryan, cl'k,	1,789
To Mark Clark,	1,789
To William Street,	1,789
To Abraham Cowley,	500
To Agnes Homes, sexton,	536
To Elenor Williams,	536
To John Shoemaker,	500
To the Church Wardens,	344
To Benjamin Goode,	1,000
To Mary Allen, her fon an idot,	500
To William Ford,	500
To Lemmy Childers,	500

To John Liptrott,	1,000
To Richard Moon, for the care of John Lee,	500
To Sufannah Morton,	1,000
To Elizabeth Dolton, for the care of John Liggon's wife,	500
To Mary Walters,	500
To the Church Wardens, for Margaret Childers,	500
To Sarah Walton,	500
To the Church Wardens, for Mary Lefter,	536
To the Collector's Commiffions,	2,218
To Ly in the hands of the Church Wardens,	2,294
	36,981

Cr.

By 1,761 Tiths, at 21 per Pole,	36,981

Ordered, That the Church Wardens pay Jeffe Burton feven pounds ten fhillings and four pence, for Providing for John Aldy's orphans.

Ryland Randolph and Thomas Adams, Gent., are chofen Church Wardens for the enfuing year.

Ordered, That the prefent Church Wardens fettle with Colo. Richard Randolph and Mr. Samuel Duvall, late Church Wardens, for year 1759 and 1760, and that they return an Acco't of the fame to the next Veftry.

Richard Adams,[25] Gent., is chofen a Veftry man in the room of William Randolph, dec'd.

Ordered, That the Sherriff collect of each Tith, twenty-one pounds of tob'o for the ufe of the Parrifh.

THOS. ADAMS,
RY. RANDOLPH.

AT A VESTRY, held at Richmond Town, October 4th, 1762.

Prefent.

The Rev'd Miles Selden, Rich'd Randolph, Bowler Cocke, Jun'r, Wm. Lewis, John Ellis, Samuel Duval, Ryland Randolph and Richard Adams, Gent., Veftrymen.

Henrico Parifh,	*Dr.*
To the Rev'd Miles Selden,	17,150
To John Bryan, clk.,	1,789
To Mark Clark, Junr.,	1,789
To William Street,	1,789
To Fortu. Sydnor, Clerk of Veftry,	500
To Agnes Homes, fexton,	536
To Elenor Williams,	536
To John Shoemaker,	536
To the Church Wardens,	344
To Benjamin Goode,	500
To Mary Allen, for her Son, an Ideot,	1,000
To William Ford,	500
To Lemmy Childers,	500
To John Liptrott,	500
To Richard Moore, for the care of John Lee,	1,000
To Sufanna Morton,	700
To Eliza. Dalton, for the care of Jno. Ligon's wife,	1,000
To Mary Walters,	1,000
To the Ch. W'dns, for Margaret Childers,	500
To do., for Mary Lefter,	500
To Philemon Childris,	500
To Eliza. Eales,	700
To a Serv't woman, named Catharine, belonging to Wm. Jones' eftate,	500
To the Collector's Commiffions,	2,638
To Thos. Rice,	500
To remain in Ch. W'dns hands,	5,468
	43,975

Cr.,

By 1,759 Tithables at 25 lbs. per Polls,	43,975

Ryland Randolph and Richard Adams, Gent., are chofen Ch. W'dns for the County, for the enfuing year.

Ordered, That the Ch. W'dns pay Jeffe Burton thirteen

pounds four fhill's and three pence half penny for providing for orphans of John Alday, dec'd.

Ordered, That the Ch. W'dns pay Richard Adams his acco. ag't the Parifhoners, of Five pounds thirteen fhillings and three pence half penny.

Ordered, That the Ch. W'dns pay Sam'l Duval his acco. for providing for Jofeph Sayer.

Ordered, That the Ch. W'dns pay Ryland Randolph his acco.

Ordered, That the Ch. W'dns pay Robert Elliott thirty fhillings, for burying a man.

Ordered, That the Ch. W'dns purchafe a Silver Cup and Salver of the fize of that at Richmond Church, for the ufe of Deep Run Church.

Ordered, That the Ch. W'dns collect of every Tithable perfon in this County 25 lbs. Tob'o, for the ufe of the Parifh, and in cafe of refufal or delay, that they make diftrefs according to law.

RICHARD ADAMS,
RY. RANDOLPH.

Teste:
FORTU. SYDNOR,
Cl'k Veftry.

AT A VESTRY, held at Richmond Town, Henrico County, on Monday, 24th day of October, 1763.

Prefent.

The Rev'd Miles Selden, Richard Randolph, Bowler Cocke, Jun'r, William Lewis, John Ellifs, Samuel Duval, Ryland Randolph and Richard Adams, Gent., Veftrymen.

The Parifh,	*Dr.*
To the rev'd Miles Selden,	17,150
To John Bryan, clk.,	1,789
To Mark Clark, clk.,	1,789
To William Street, clerk,	1,789
To Fortu. Sydnor, Clerk Veftry,	500
To Agnes Homes, Sexton,	536

To Elenor Williams, for cleaning church,	536
To Jno. Ellis, who is app'd sexton to deep Run Church,	536
To the Ch. W'ds,	344
To Ben. Goode,	500
To John Liptrot,	800
To Richard Moore, for Jno. Lee,	1,200
To Sufa. Morton,	800
To Eliza. Dalton, for ——— Ligon's wife,	1,000
To Mary Walters,	1,000
To Margaret Childers,	500
To the Ch. W'dns, for Mary Lefter,	500
To Thomas Conway and Wife,	1,000
To Philemon Childers,	500
To Catharine McBurnet,	500
To Thomas Rice,	500
To John Jones and Wife,	1,000
To Mary Franklin,	800
To Jane Porter,	300
To prudence Williamfon, for the fupport of her children,	1,000
To John Weft,	500
To John Clarkfon,	50
Aron Freeman, exempted from paying Parifh Levy,	
Jno. Enroughty, for himfelf and fon,	1,000
To James Whitlow, for Wm. Reins,	800
To the Ch. W'dns, for John Conway,	300
To Alex'r Robinfon, for James Conway,	500
To Judith Blackbone,	500
To Miles Redford, 4 ℔s. twice lifted,	84
To Martha Redford, for 2 do.,	42
To John Oakley, for One do.,	21
To Lewis Hancock, for 3 do.,	63
To William Morris, for 1 do.,	25
To Jno Ragland,[26] for 1 do.,	25
To William Smith, for 1 do.,	25
To John John Shepherd, for 5 do.,	125
To Collector's Commiffions,	2,977
To remain the Ch. W'dns Hands,	5,465
	49,851

Cr.

By the Shff. for Tith's twice Lifted,	225
By 1,838 Tiths, at 27 ℔ per Poll,	49,626
	49,851

Cafh,	*Dr.*		
	£.	s.	d.
To the Rev'd Miles Selden, his Acco.,	12	17	9
To Nich's Sherrer, his do.,		10	6
To Jeffee Burton, for Allday's Orphans,	18	13	0
To Thomas Wilkinfon, for Conway,	3	0	0
To Ryland Randolph, as Ch. W'dn, as per acco.	34	1	8
To do., for fmall pox negro,	2	17	0
	93	19	11
Cr.			
By Ball'nce, Ch. W'dns hands,	55	1	0
By Richard Randolph,	2	5	0
By Ch. W'dns, for fines,	3	10	0
By Ryland Randolph, for Sarah Doane, do.,	2	10	0
Balance due from Parifh,	30	13	11
To do., for their cloths that was burnt,	22	0	0
	93	19	11

Richard Randolph and Rich'd Adams are chofen Ch. W'dns for the enfuing year.

The Sheriff is appointed Collector of the levy.

Ordered, That he give Bond at next Court of that he collect of every Tithable perfon in the County 27 ℔s. n't tob'o.

Signed,

RYLAND RANDOLPH,
RICHARD ADAMS.

Tefte:

FORTU. SYDNOR,
C. V.

AT A VESTRY, held at Richmond Town, On Thurfsday, the 10th October, 1764.

Prefent.

The Rev'd Miles Selden, Rich'd Randolph, Bowler Cocke, William Lewis, John Ellis, Jo. Lewis, Samuel Duval, Ryland Randolph and Richard Adams, Gent., Veft. Men.

To the Rev'd Mr. Selden,	17,150
To John Bryan,	1,789
To Mark Clark,	1,789
To Fortu. Sydnor,	500
To Wm. Street,	1,789
To Agnes Homes, Sexton,	536
To Elenor Williams, do.,	536
To Jos. Ellis, do.,	536
To Ch. W'dns,	344
To Ben. Goode,	500
To John Liptrott,	800
To Richard Moore, for Jno. Lee,	800
To Sufannah Morton,	800
To Eliza. Dalto, for Ligon's Wife,	1,000
To Mary Walter,	1,000
To Margaret Childers,	500
To Ch. Wardens, for Mary Lefter,	500
To Thomas Conaway and wife,	1,000
To Philemon Childers,	1,000
To Catherine McBurnet,	500
To Thomas Rice,	500
To Mary Frankling,	800
To Jane Porter,	800
To Prudence Williamfon, for sup't of children,	1,000
To John Weft,	500
To Ch. Wardens, for Wm. Reins,	300
To John Enroughty, for son,	300
To John Conaway, for keeping Thomas Conaway,	100
To Judith Blackboard, for her two Bas. children,	500
To Winfrey Wright, Exempted from pay'g Parifh levies for the future,	
To Jno. Grimftead, for sup't of his wife,	500

To Elizabeth Lucas,	500
To Ann Spurlock,	500
To William Hogg,	500
To Thomas Williams, for removing Sarah and Thomas Roberts,	120
To David Atkins, for Sally Turner's bas. child,	500
To Eliza. Eales,	500
	40,689
To Sheriff, for 21 Infolvents,	533
To Jofeph Parfons, for 16 Tyths, twice enlifted,	423
	46,032
By 1,918 Tiths, at 24 lbs. Tob'o, To Cr. per Poll,	46,032

The Sheriff appt. Col. of this levy, and to give bond.

Bowler Cocke and Samuel Duval, Gents., appointed Ch. W'dns.

Ordered, that the Ch. W'dns have proper feats where wanting at the Churches in this Parifh.

Ballance in the hands of former Ch. Wardens, as per Acc't to be paid the prefent Ch. Wardens, £12, 6, 11.

Teft:

B. COCKE, Junr.,
SAML. DU VAL.

The Parifh, *Dr.*

	lbs. Tob'o.
To the Rev'd Mr. Selden, his Annual Sallary,	17,157
To Jno. Bryan, Clk, Richmond Church. his do.,	1,789
To William Street, Clk, Deep Run Church, his do.,	1,789
To James Sharp, reader at Curl's Church, his do.,	1,789
To Agnes Hoomes, Sexton,	536
To Jofeph Ellis, Sexton,	536
To Fortu. Sydnor, Clk Veftry,	536
To the Ch. W'dns,	344
To do., for Mary Lefter,	500
To Benja. Goode,	500

To Sufa. Morton,	500
To Eliza. Dalton,	800
To Mary Walters,	1,000
To Margaret Childers,	1,000
To Mary Conway,	500
To Philemon Childers,	700
To Catherine McBurnet,	1,000
To Thomas Rice,	500
To Mary Franklin,	500
To Jane Porter,	800
To prudence Williamfon,	800
To John Weft,	1,000
To Jno. Enroughty, for fon,	1,000
To Ch. W'dns, for Wm. Rives,	500
To Judith Blackbond, for her and baf'd children,	300
To John Grimftead, for his Wife,	500
To Eliza. Lucas,	500
To Ann Spurlock,	500
To Wm. Hogg,	500
To Daniel Atkins, for Sally Turner's B. child,	500
To Mary Bridgman, widow, for her children	500
To the Ch. W'dns, for Margaret Brown,	600
To the Ch. W'dns, for Jno. Jones,	750
To Eleanor Williams,	500
To Samuel Thompfon, payable to Ch. W'dns,	500
To Hayes Whitlow, for William Clark,	500
To the Rev'd Mr. Selden, for 2 tiths twice lifted,	300
To Eliza McCallum, for Ann O'Brien, 8 months,	48
To John Branfford, for do., laft year,	300
To Sher's Com's, for Collecting,	2,824
To remain Sheriff's hands,	1,164
	47,075

Cr.

By 1,887 Tiths, at 25 ℔s. per Poll,	47,075

By Ball., in the Hands of former Ch. W'dns, £15, 20.
Ord'd, That Ch. W'dns pay Jno. Price his acc't, £2, 18, 4.

The Baptismal Font.

Ord'd, That the Ch. W'dns, pay Jno. Barnes his acco., £3, 7, 6.

Philip Watfon, Daniel Price and Nathaniel Wilkinfon, are chofen Veftryman; Phil. Watfon, in the room of Thos. Adams, who is removed out of the Parifh; Dan'l Price, in the room of John Povall, dec'd; and Nathaniel Wilkinfon in the room of Robt. Mofby, who has refigned.

Richard Randolph and Joseph Lewis, Gent., are appointed Ch. W'dns for the enfuing year.

Jofeph Lewis is appointed Collector of this levy, to give bond to Ch. W'dns.

RICHARD RANDOLPH,
JOSEPH LEWIS.

AT A VESTRY, held at the Court Houfe of Henrico County, on Wednesday, the 22d day of Oct'br, 1766, for laying the Parifh levy, prefent—the Rev'd Miles Selden, Richard Randolph, Jofeph Lewis, Rich'd Adams, Bowler Cocke, Ryland Randolph, Daniel Price and Samuel Duval, Veftrymen.

The Parifh,	*Dr.*
To the Rev'd Mr. Selden, on his Annual Sallary,	17,150
To John Bryan, clk Rich'd Church,	1,789
To William Street, clk Deep run,	1,789
To Jofeph Sharp, Clerk Curl's,	1,789
To Agnefs Homes, Sexton,	536
To Eleanor Williams, Sexton,	536
To Jofeph Ellis, Sexton,	536
To Fortu. Sydnor, clk Veftry,	500
To the Ch. W'dns,	344
To do., for Mary Lefter,	500
To do., for Margaret Brown,	750
To do., John Jones,	500
To Benj. Goode,	500
To Sufa. Morton,	800
To Eliza. Dalton, for Ligon's Wife,	1,000
To Mary Walker,	1,000
To Margaret Childers,	500
To Mary Conway,	1,000

To Mary Bridgman,	600
To Catharine McBurnett,	500
To Thomas Rice,	500
To Mary Frankling,	800
To Jane Porter,	800
To prudence Williamfon,	1,000
To Jno. Weft,	800
To John Enroughty, for his fon and felf,	1,000
To Jno. Grimftead, for his Wife,	500
To Eliza Lucas,	500
To Ann Surlock,	500
To Wm. Hogg,	1,000
To David Atkins, for Sally Turner's Baftard,	500
To Eleanor Williams,	500
To the Ch. W'dns, for Sam'l Thomfon,	500
To the Ch. W'dns, for Wm. Reins,	300
To Judith Blackbond, (pay'ble Ch. W'dns,) for her children,	500
To Elza McCallum, for Ann Obrien,	300
To Margery Barnes,	500
To Amos Liptrot,	500
To Jno. Clark, for Burying Phil's children,	150
To Roger Cocke Bailey, for Jemima Scott,	150
To Collectors Com's, at 6 per ct.,	2,856
To a Deposit in Ch. W'dns hands,	825
	47,600
By 1,904 Tith's, @ 25 ℔s. per Poll,	47,600

John Randolph,[27] is chofen a Veftryman in the room of Philip Watfon, dec'd.

Thos. Robinfon and Benja. Clark, are exempted from paying Parifh Levys.

By Ballance in the Hands of prefent Ch. W'dns, £2, 2, 42.

Richard Randolph and Jos. Lewis, Gent., Chose Ch. W'dns for the Enfuing year.

Jos. Lewis, Sher., Appointed Collector of this Levy.

RICHARD RANDOLPH,
JOSEPH LEWIS.

AT A VESTRY, held at the Court Houfe, on Wednefday, the 14 Day of October, 1767, for Laying the Parifh Levy, Prefent—The Rev'd Mr. Selden, Wm. Lewis, Bowler Cocke, Jos. Lewis, Richard Adams, Ryland Randolph, Dan'l Price and Nath'l Wilkinfon.

The Parifh,	*Dr.*
To the Rev'd Mr. Selden, his Sallary,	17,150
To Jno. Bryan,	1,789
To Wm. Street,	1,786
To James Sharp,	1,789
To Agnes Homes, as Sexton,	536
To Eleanor Williams, Sexton,	536
To Fortu. Sydnor, Clk proc'g year,	536
To the Ch. W'dns for Church Ex's,	344
To Mary Lefter,	1,000
To Wm. Reins,	400
To Margaret Brown,	300
To John Jones,	500
To Sam'l Thompfon,	500
To Benja. Goode,	500
To Eliza. Dalton, for Liggon's Wife,	400
To Margaret Childers,	800
To Catha. McBurnet,	400
Thos. Rice,	250
To Mary Franklin,	400
To Jane Porter,	650
To prudence Williamfon, for her children,	800
To Jno. Weft,	600
To John Enroughty, for himfelf and Son,	600
To Judith Blackbond,	800
To John Grimftead, for his Wife,	500
To Eliza Lucas,	500
To Ann Spurlock,	400
To Wm. Hogg,	400
To David Atkins, for Sally Turner's Child,	750
To Mary Bridgwater,	400
To Eleanor Williams,	500
To Margery Barnes,	400

To Amos Liptrot,	400
To Rich'd Moore,	400
To Eliza. Eales, R. Cottrell, laft year,	400
To Eliza. Eales,	700
To Nath'l Bridgwater, for his Wife,	800
To John Price, Eliza. Porter's Baftard Children,	300
To the Ch. W'dns, for the Thos. Jeff's Wife and Children,	400
To Collectors Commiffions, @ 6 p. ct.	2,491
To Catharine Freeman,	600
	44,010

Cr.

By 1,903 Ths., @ 23 ℔s. per poll,	43,769
Ball. due the Collect.,	241
	44,010

By Ball. in Hands of Jos. Lewis, Ch. W'dns, 2, 17, 02.

On pet. Thos. Alley, he is Set Parifh Levy free.

George Cox, App'd a Veftryman, in the Room of Peter Randolph, Efq'r, dec'd.

Richard Adams and Ryland Randolph, Gent., Chofen Ch. W'dns the enfuing year.

The Ch. W'dns are App'd Collectors of the Levy.

Purfuant to an Act of Affembly and in Obedience to an Order of Henrico Court, the Veftry do divide the parifh into precincts, and Appoint perfons to proceffion every perfons land, as follows:

Richard Cottrell, Jos. Brown, Thos. Ellis and Wm. Ellis, to proceffion from the mouth of Great Weftham to William Gordon's, thence up Between Gordon's Road and Jas. River, to the Head of the Parifh.

2.

William Winfton, Thos. Owen, Thos. Wilkinfon and William Bacon, from Gordon's road to the Head of the Parifh, thence to Chickahominy Swamp, and down that to the Head of Upland Brook and thence to Gordon's aforef'd.

3.

Wm. Jones, Jno. Mofby, Fras. Cornet and Jos. Britton, from Chickahominy Swamp and Upland Brook to the Head of f'd Brook.

4.

John Pleafants, Sam'l Williamfon, Martin Burton, and Drewry Wood, Between Chickahominy Swamp and the Brook road, as Low as Cannon's and Smith's Mill.

Jacob Smith, Drury Brazeal, Wm. New and John Wood, between the Mouth of Gilley's Creek and Great Weftham, and from Cannon and Gordon's to the River.

6.

Edward Curd, Jno. Harwood, Jas. Cocke and Jacob Pleafants, from the mouth of Gilley's Creek to Jos. Lewif's, on Chickahominy Swamp, and up as far as Cannon Smith's Mill.

7.

Nich's Giles, Matthew Herbert, John Whitlow and Jos. Whitlock, jr., Between Gilley's' and Cornelius Creek from the River to the Seven Pines road, and as Low as the Southern Branch Bridge.

8.

Jofiah Bullington, Jno. Burton, Thomas Jordan, Jr., and Robt. Atkins, between Corneliuf's and four Mile Creek, the Main County road and the River.

9.

Milner Redford, Jno. Redford, William Parker and Richard Sharpe, between Two mile Creek, four Mile Creek, the Main Road and the River.

10.

William Frayfer, William Whitlow, William Bullington and Richard Whitlow, between Corneliuf's and four Mile Creek, from the Main road to the Seven Pines road.

11.

Julius Allen, Anthony Matthews, Robert Spiers and Jacob

Faris, between Jos. Lewif's and Boar Swamp, on Chickahominy, to the Head of Boar Swamp.

12.

Jno. Carter, Jno. Hales, Benja. Jordan and William Faris, from the mouth of Boar Swamp to the County Line, on Chickahominy, and back to the Long Bridge road.

13.

Sam'l Gathright, William Hobfon, Thos. Childrey and John Gathright, between Four mile Creek, Bailey's Run and White Oak Swamp.

14.

Chas. Woodfon, Robert Pleafants, Robert Pleafants, Jr., Thos. Pleafants and Jno. Martin, Between Bailey's Run, the County Line and the Weftern Branch.

15.

Humphrey Smith, John Royfter, Thos. Rogers and Thos. Jolley, Between the Head of Bailey's Run, the Weftern Runn, and the County Line, as far North as the Fork of the Long Bridge road; and, it is Ordered, That the f'd proceffioners Return an Account of their proceedings According to law.

RICH'D ADAMS,
RY. RANDOLPH.

AT A VESTRY, held in the Court Houfe of Henrico County, on Wednesday, the 9th day of November, 1768, for laying the Parifh Levy.

Prefent.

The Rev'd Miles Selden, Rich'd Randolph, Jno. Ellis, Sam'l Duval, Bowler Cocke, Ryland Randolph, Jos. Lewis, Dan'l Price, Nathaniel Wilkinson.[28] Geo. Cox Took the Oath required by Law. Pref't, G. Cox.

The Parifh of Henrico,	*Dr.*
To the Rev'd Miles Selden, his Annual Sallary,	17,150
To John Bryan, clerk,	1,789
To William Street, do.,	1,789

To Jas. Sharp, do.,	1,789
To Agnes Homes, Sexton Curl's Church,	536
To Rich'd Williams, who is app'd do., R. Church,	536
To Jos. Ellis, do., Deep Run do.,	536
To Fortun. Sydnor, Clk Veftry,	500
To the C. W'dns, for Elem'ts,	300
To do., for Mary Lefter,	
To do., for Margaret Brown,	
To do., for Samuel Thompfon,	
To Benja. Goode,	
To Eliza. Dalton, for Liggon's Wife,	
To Margaret Childers,	
To Catharine Burnet,	
To Thomas Rice,	
To Jno. Weft,	
To Jno. Enroughty and his fon,	
To Jno. Grimftead, for his wife,	
To Eliza. Lucas,	
To Ann Spurlock,	
To Wm. Hogg,	
To Mary Bridgman,	
To Eleanor Williams,	
To Margery Barnes,	
To Amos Liptrot,	
To Richard Moore,	
To Nath'l Bridgwater, for his wife,	
To the Ch. W'dns, for the poor of the Parifh,	25,000
To Solo. Fuffel, for taking care of Eliza. Carter and her two children, Eight weeks,	300
To Nich's Conway, for a Tith 2d lifted,	23
To Abra. Bailey, for Maint'g Jemima Scott 2 years,	500
To Wm. Smith, for do., Jno. Burnet 13 days,	150
To Wm. Robinfon, Confta., for Conv'g 7 paupers do., to Chesterfield,	48
To do., for a Woman, Margaret Mackmaham, (bel'g to to K. Queen,) and four children to Hanover,	160
To do., for 2 levies in 1767 and 1766,	48
To James Lindfey, Confta., for do.,	48

To James Allen, for 14 Infov'ts, for 1767 @ 23 ℔s. Tob'o,	322
To Abra. Baley, for David Johnfton,	300
To Geo. Scherrer, for Burying a Poor Woman,	100
To Geo. Donald, for Burying a Poor Woman,	100
To Sam'l Shepherd, for Catharine Freeman,	40
To Mark Woodcock, for 7 Tiths 2ce lifted,	161
To Jos. Whitlock, for 1 do.,	23
To Rich'd Williams, for mending Surplis,	30
To Jno. Barnes, for Margery Barnes,	200
To Wm. Morris, for Burying Eliza Lucas,	100
	52,578
To Collectors Com's, @ 6 per ct.,	3,154
	55,732
By 2,012 Tiths, @ 28 ℔s. per Poll,	56,336
By a Depofition in Collectors Hands,	604

It is the Opinion of the Veftry, that Curl's Church be removed, and that Richard and George Cox, Samuel Duval, Jos. Lewis, Nath'l Wilkinfon and Thos. Watkins, Gent., or any five of them, view the moft convenient place to Build one on, and that they make Report to the next Veftry, to be held for laying the Parifh Levy.

Ord'd, Richard Randolph fend for filver falver and 1 pint zD Silver Cup, for the ufe of D. Runn Church.

By Ball'ce in the Hands of Richard Adams, p. 17, 12.

Ord., Ch. W'dns pay Jno. Clarkfon 3 7-12 for prov'g for Thos. Rice 3 months.

Richard Randolph and Samuel Duval, Gent., are Chofen Ch. W'dns for Enfuing year.

Jas. Allen and Jno. Royfter are app'd Collectors of this levy, to give Bonds to the C'lk Veftry.

RICHARD RANDOLPH,
SAM. DU VAL.

In Obedience to an Order of Veftry, we have Proceffioned

all the Lines and Bounds of the Lands as we were directed, which were as follows:

The Lines between fore mile Creek, two mile Creek, Mane road and river.

The Lines between John Pleafants and Francis Epes agreed.

The Lines between John Pleafants and John Sharpe agreed.

The Lines between John Pleafants and Milner Redford agreed.

The Lines between Robt. Pleafants and Jofeph Woodfon agreed.

The Lines between John and Milner Redford agreed.

The Lines between William C. Redford and Arche filbard agreed.

The Lines between John and William Frayfer agreed.

The Lines between William Frayfer and Hays Whitlo agreed.

The Lines between John Pleafants and Francis Pearce Juft Agreed.

Proceffioned by

JOHN REDFORD,
MILNER REDFORD,
WM. PARKER,
RICH'D SHARPE.

FEBRUARY 29th, 1768.

In Obedience to an Order of the Henrico Veftry, we have proceffioned the Lands in our Precinct, from Gilley's Creek to the Weftham—only the lands of William Wills, the Parties not appearing to fhow the lines between.

Given under hands.

JACOB SMITH,
DRURY BRAZEAL,
WM. NEW,
JOHN WOOD.

In Obedience to the within Order, we have proceffioned all the Lands within our Precincts, all the Parties agreed.

RICHARD COTTRELL,
THOMAS ELLIS,
WILLIAM ELLIS,
JOSEPH BROWN.

Purfuant to an Order of Veftry, to us directed, We, the fubfcribers, have gone in proceffion and renewed the Bounds of the feveral Tracts of Land within the Limmits to us Profcribed, Being in prefence and with the confent of the proprietors of faid land.

Witnefs our hand this 13th day of February, 1768.

JOHN PLEASANTS,
DRURY WOOD,
MARTIN BURTON,
SAM'L WILLIAMSON.

Purfuant to an Order of Veftry, to us directed, We, the fubfcribers, have gone in proceffion, in Preference and with confent of the Parties, have renewed the Several Lines within the Bounds prefcribed in faid Order. Given under our hands this Twenty-firft day of March, one thoufand feven hundred and sixty-eight.

EDWARD CURD, Sen'r,
JOHN HARWOOD, Sen'r,
JAMES COCKE, Jun'r,
JACOB PLEASANTS.

In Obedience to an Order of Veftry, hereto annexed, we have peacably proceffioned all Lines in our Precinct, the Parties being prefent.

SAMUEL GATHRIGHT,
WM. HOPSON,
THOS. CHILDREY,
JNO. GATHRIGHT.

In Compliance with the Orders of Henrico County Court, For Proceffioning the Lands between Cornelius Creek and two mile Creek, the main County road and river, We proceffioned the Lines between Lizby Turpin and Jofeph Bailey, and between Lizby Turpin and Richard Reynards, and between Richard Reynard, and Jofeph Bailey—Richard Reynard and Jos. Bailey, prefent; alfo the Lines between Abraham Bailey and Jofeph Bailey—both parties Prefent; and between Hays Whitlow and Jonathan Williams—both parties prefent; Between Jofiah Bullington and John Burton—

both partys prefent; and between Jofiah Bullington and William Burton—both parties prefent; and Between Jeffee Burton and John Burton—both parties prefent; and Between George Cox and William Burton—both Parties prefent; and between George Cox and Epps—both parties prefent; and between Mary Stewart and Randolph Leonard—Ward and Nicholas Giles prefent; and between George Cox and William Perkins—both Parties Prefent; between George Cox and Thomas Jordone, Jun'r—both Parties prefent; between Wm. Perkins and Josias Bullington—both parties Prefent; between Wm. Barker and Randolph—both parties Prefent; Between Stewart's and Epps—Both prefent.

JOHN BURTON,
JOSIAH BULLINGTON,
THOS. JORDON, Jun'r,
ROBT. ADKINS.

AT A VESTRY, held at the Court Houfe, on Monday, the 16th Day of April, 1770, for Laying the Parifh Levy.

Prefent.

Richard Randolph, Bowler Cocke, Ryland Randolph, Sam'l Duval, Jos. Lewis, Rich'd Adams and George Cox, Gent., Veftrymen.

The Parifh,	*Dr.*
To the Rev'd Mr. Selden, his Annual Sall'y,	17,150
To John Bryan, clk Richmond Church,	1,789
To Wm. Street, clk Deep Run do.,	1,789
To Jas. Sharp, do. Curl's,	1,789
To Agnes Homes, Sexton Curl's,	536
To Rich'd Williams, do. Richmond Church,	536
To Jos. Ellis, do. of Deep Run Church,	536
To Fortu. Sydnor, Clk Veftry,	536
To the Ch. W'dns, for Church Elem'ts,	300
To Jas. Royal, for keep'g J. Black bas. child,	500
Prest. Jno. Randolph,	
To Thos. Alley and Wife,	400
To Sam'l Thompfon,	300

To Hannah Clark,	300
To the Ch. W'dns, for Matt. Bridgman,	300
To the do., for Margaret Childers,	300
To do., Margaret Brown,	300
To do., Eliza. Dalton, for Liggon's Wife,	600
To do., Thos. Rice,	400
To do., for Jno. Weft and his daughter Molly,	600
To Jno. Grimftead, for his wife,	300
To Ch. W'dns, for Ann Spurlock,	500
To Ch. W'dns, for Wm. Hogg,	500
To Mary Bridgman, for herfelf and child,	500
To Nath'l Bridgwater and wife,	600
To Anto. Matthews, for Eliza Childers,	300
To the Ch. W'dns, for Robt. Scott,	300
To do., for Aaron Freeman and wife,	300
To Henry Brittain,	300
	32,561
To Com's for collecting,	2,274
	34,835
To a Depofition in Ch. W'dns hands,	3,073
	37,908

Cr.

By 2,106 Tiths, @ 18 pr. Poll,	37,908

Ord'd, Ch. W'dns pay Jas. Vaughn four pounds, for providing for Margaret Brown 8 months.

Ord'd, Ch. W'dns pay Thos. Watkins £3, 3, 0, for David Johnfon.

The Order of laft Veftry, for the removal of Curl's Church cont'd, and Wm Lewis and Rich'd Adams, Gent., are added to f'd order.

Richard Adams and Geo. Cox. Gent., are chofen Ch. W'dns for the enfuing year.

Ord'd, Ch. W'dns Lett to loweft bidder the inclofing of the

land belonging the Church at Richmond, with Saw'd Pofts and rails in the Beft workmanlike manner.

Ord'd, That Richard Randolph and Sam'l Duval, Gent., former Ch. W'dns, pay the Ballance of Ninety-four pounds Nineteen Shillings and ½ to Ballance of due from the (to the Parifh) to Rich'd Adams and Geo. Cox, Gent., the pref'g Ch. W'dns.

Geo. Cox, Gent., is app'd Coll'r of this Levy.

RICH'D ADAMS,
GEORGE COX.

AT A VESTRY, held at Richmond, on Thurfday, the 25th Day of November, 1770, for Laying the Parifh Levy.

Prefent.

The Rev. Miles Selden, Wm. Lewis, Jos. Lewis,
John Ellis, Ryland Randolph, Geo. Cox,
Sam'l Duval, Rich'd Adams,
Richard Randolph, Gents., Veftrymen.

The Parifh,	*Dr.*
To the Rev'd Miles Selden, his Annual Sallery,	17,150
To Wm. Street, Clk of deep run,	1,789
To Jos. Sharp, do., Curl's,	1,789
To John Bryan, do. Richmond,	536
To Agnes Homes, sexton at Curl's Church,	536
To Rich'd Wm'fon, do. to Richmond Church,	536
To Jos. Elis, do. Deep Run,	500
To Fortu. Sydnor, Clk Veftry,	300
To Church Wardens, for Church elements,	500
To Thos. Alley and Wife,	500
To Hannah Clark,	500
To Ch. W'dns, for Matt. Bridgman,	500
To do., for Marg't Childers,	700
To do., for Mary Brown,	50
To do., for Eliza. Dalton, for Liggon's Wife,	1,000
To do., for Thos. Rice,	600
To do., for Jno. Weft and his daughter Molly,	600

To John Grimftead, for his wife,	500
To Ch. W'dns, for Ann Spurlock,	800
To do., for Wm. Hogg,	800
To do., for Nath'l Bridwater, for his wife,	600
To do., for Eliza. Childers,	600
To Ch. W'dns, for Aaron Freeman's Wife,	600
To do., for Henry Brittain's Wife,	600
To do., for Catharine McBurnet,	500
To do., for Benja. Goode,	600
To do., for John Jones,	600
To do., for Mary Franklin,	600
To do., for Mary Swinton,	600
To do., for Richard Moore,	500
To John Enroughty, for felf and fon,	1,000
To Sheriff's Com'ns for Collecting,	2,389
	42,214
To the Depofitam,	146
	42,360

Cr.

By 2,118 Tiths, @ 20 per Poll,	42,360

It is agreed that the Ch. W'dns pay unto Mary Thomfon one pound feven fhillings, for Burying her hufband.

Richard Adams and George Cox, Gent., are Chofen Church wardens for the Enfuing year.

Ord'd, That the prefent Church W'ds do fettle with R'd Randolph and Sam'l Duval, Gent., former Church wardens, for the money that is due in their hands, and in cafe refufal or delay of payment, that they commence fuit againft them for the Ball'ce in their hands.

Ord'd, That the Ch. W'ds do let to the Loweft bidder the Walling in of the Richmond Church Yard w'th Bricks, 4 foot and ½ high above ground, to the Loweft bidder, includ'g the Land bel'g to the Church.

Ord'd, That the Ch. W'ds agree with any perfon for the Cure of Pridgeon Waddle's Nofe—not exceed'g ten pounds.

Turner Southall, Gent., is chofen Veftryman in the room of John Randolph, Gent.

RICHARD ADAMS,
GEORGE COX.

AT A VESTRY, held at the Court Houfe, on Monday, the 8th day of July, 1771, for Appointing Proceffioners of the Bounds of every Perfons land in the Parifh and County of Henrico.

Prefent.

Richard Randolph, Wm. Lewis, Sam'l Duval, Richard Adams, Dan'l Price, Nath'l Wilkinfon, George Cox, Veftrymen.

Purfuant to an Act of Affembly, and in Obedience to an order of Henrico Court, this Veftry do now divide the parifh into precincts, and appoint perfons to proceffion every perfons Land in f'd Parifh.

No. 1.

Richard Cottrell, Jos. Brown, Jeffe Ellis, William Ellis, Sam'l Shepherd, Jos. Ellis—from the mouth of Great Weft Ham to William Gordon's, thence up between Gordon's road and James river, to the head of the Parifh.

No. 2.

Thos. Owin, Dabney Pettus, Sam'l Williamfon and Wm. Miller—from the fork of the Brook and Swamp, thence up the Brook to Gordon's Road, thence to the Head of Hungary Branch, thence to Turner's Runn, thence down the Run to Chick'y Swamp, and down the Swamp to the Beginning.

3.

Wm. Jones, John Mofby, Eran's Cornet, Jos. Brittain—from Chickahominy Swamp and Upland Brook to the head of the faid Brook.

4.

Jno. Pleafants, Carp'r, Sam'l Williamfon, Martin Burton and Drury Wood—Between Chickahominy Swamp and the Brook Road, as low as Kennon's & Smith's Mill.

5.

Edward Curd, John Harwood, Jas. Cocke, and Jacob Pleafants—from the Mouth of Gilley's Creek to Jos. Lewif's, on Chickahominy Swamp, and up as far as Kennon & Smith's Mill.

6.

Nich's Giles, Matthew Herbett, Jno. Whitlow, Jas. Whitlow—Between Gilley's Creek and Corneliuf's, from the River to the Seven Pines Road, and as low down as the Southern Branch Bridge.

7.

Jofiah Bullington, Jno. Burton, Thos. Jordon, Jr., and Rob't Adkins—between Corneliuf's and two Mile Creek, the Main Country Road and River.

8.

James Hallock, Richard Throgmorton, Wm. Parker, Rich'd Sharp—between two Mile Creek, from four Mile Creek, the Main road and river.

9.

Benja. Johnfon, David Bowles, Michael Johnfon, Nath'l Holman, Wm. Shepherd and Benja. Shepherd—from the head of Turner's Runn to Hungry Branch, thence to Gordon's Road, to the County Line, thence along that Line to Chickahominy Swamp, thence down the Swamp to Turner's Runn.

10.

Jacob Smith, Wm. New and Sam'l Price, Lewis Ball, Leonard Henley, and Jno. Hodge and John Wood—between the Mouth of Gilley's Creek and Great Weftham, and from Kennon's and Gordon's to the River.

11.

Thos. Goode, William Whitlow, Jos. Goode, Jno. Lindfay, and Edw'd Wade and Geo. Robertfon—between Corneliuf's and four Mile Creek, from the Main Road to the 7 Pines Road.

12.

Charles Allen, Anthony Matthews, Robert Spears, Jacob Faris, Ifham Allen and James Valentine—between Jos. Lewis' and Boar Swamp, on Chickahominy to the head of Boar Swamp.

13.

Jno. Carter, Wm. Faris, Wm. Gathright, (fon of Eph'a,) Thos. Watkins, Jr., Robt. Jordan and Geo. Baker—from the Mouth of Boar Swamp to the County Line on Chickahominy, and back to the Long Bridge Road.

14.

Sam'l Gathright, William Hopfon, Thos. Childrey and John Gathright—between Four Mile Creek, Bailey's Run and White Oak Swamp.

15.

Robert Pleafants, Robert Pleafants, Jr., Thos. Pleafants, Thos. Eldridge and Rob't Poval—Between Bailey's Runn, the County Line and the Weftern Branch.

16.

Thos. Rogers, Thos. Jolley and William Binford—between the head of Bailey's Run, the Weftern Runn and the County Line, as far North as the fork of the Long Bridge Road.

Ordered, that the faid Proceffioners make their proceffions and Return an Account of their Proceedings, according to Law.

RICHARD ADAMS,
GEORGE COX.

AT A VESTRY held at Richmond Town, Henrico County, Monday, the 9th of day December, 1771, for Laying the Parifh Levy.

Prefent.

The Rev'd Miles Selden, Richard Randolph, Sam'l Duval, Richard Adams, Jofeph Lewis, Turner Southall, George Cox, Daniel Price, Gentlemen, Veftrymen.

The Parifh Henrico, *Dr.*

To the Rev'd Miles Selden, his Annual Salary,	17,150
To Wm. Street, Clerk Deep Run Church,	1,789
To Jos. Sharp, do. Curl's Church,	1,789
To John Bryan, do. Richmond,	1,789
To Agnes Holmes, Sexton at Curl's Church,	536
To Richard Wm'fon, do. at Richmond,	536
To Jos. Ellis, do. at Deep Run,	536
To Fortu. Sydnor, C'lk. Veftry Proceff'g Year,	500
To the Church Wardens, for Church Elements,	300
To Thomas Alley,	250
To Hannah Clarke,	500
To the Church wardens, for Matthew Bridgman,	500
To do. for Margaret Childers,	700
To John Grinftead, for his wife,	500
To Jno. Weft and his daughter Molly,	700
To the Church Wardens, for Ann Spurlock,	1,000
To do., for William Hogg,	1,000
To do., for Nath'l Bridgwater, for Wife,	700
To do., for Eliza. Childers,	1,000
To do., for Aarons Freeman's Wife,	1,000
To do., for Henry Britain's Wife,	800
To do., for Catherine McBurnett,	500
To do., for Benja. Goode,	600
To do., for Mary Frankling,	700
To do., for Mary Swinton,	600
To do., for Richard Moore,	500
To do., for Jno. Enroughty, for felf and fon,	1,000
To Jno. Orange,	300
To James Bowyer, for keeping Cathfton,	750
To Thomas Frankling, for keeping Mary Brown,	300
To Mrs. Abigail Richardfon, for Mary and Sufanna Jeffs, children of Sarah Jeffs, in full for the Time fhe hath kept them, and to indemnify the Parifh from all charges for keep'g and Bringing up the faid children for the time to come, they being now bound Apprentices to her,	1,500

To Abra. Baily, Conft, his Acc't allowed for removing five perfons out of this Parifh,	237
To allowed David Bowles a Levy Remitted him,	20
To Thomas Chaddock, for Burying Martha Hutton,	200
To the Church Wardens, for William Going for taking Shadrach Vaughan, Orphan, as apprentice, and indemnifying them from any farther Charge in Bringing up the s'd child,	250
To Collector's Commiffions,	3,493
To Depositam in hands Church Wardens,	13,400
	52,225

Cr.

By 2,329 Tithables, at 25 ℔. per Poll,	58,225

The Sheriff of the County is appointed Collector, and to give Bond in the Office.

Dr. to Balance Due the Church Wardens in Cafh, £22, 17, 5.

RICHARD ADAMS,
GEORGE COX.

A Return of Jno. Pleafants, Carp'r, Drury Wood, Sam'l Williamfon and Martin Burton, who were, by Order of Veftry held the 8th day of July, 1771, Appointed to Proceffion the Bounds of every perfons Land between Chickahominy Swamp and the Brook Road, as low as Kennon's & Smith's Mill.

Purfuant to an Order of the Veftry, to us directed, we, the fubfcribers, have gone in proceffion and renewed the Bounds of the Several Tracts of Lands within the Limits prefcribed by the faid order, according to Law.

JOHN PLEASANTS, Carpt.,
DRURY WOOD,
SAM'L WILLIAMSON,
MARTIN BURTON.

Teft,

FORTU. SYDNOR,
C. Veftry.

In Obedience to an Order of Veftry, we have proceffioned all the Bounds of Lands within the Bounds therein, moft of the Bounds, parties being prefent, and by Confent of thofe Abfent, who were convenient, all quietly done by us.

BEN. JOHNSON,
DAVID BOWLES,
MICHAEL JOHNSON,
WILLIAM SHEPHERD,
BENJAMIN SHEPHERD.

March 25th, 1772.

In Obedience to an Order of Veftry, we the fubfcribers, have proceffioned the Land within the within mentioned precinct, all parties Agreed. given under our hands, this 27th day of March, 1772.

JACOB SMITH,
LEWIS BALL,
LEONARD HENLEY,
JOHN WOOD.

In Obedience to an Order Veftry, appointing us, the fubfcribers, to proceffion the Lines from Weftham to Tuckahoe Creek, we have proceffioned the fame, all parties agreed. given under our hand this 6th day of April, 1772.

JOSEPH ELLIS,
SAMUEL SHEPHERD,
JOSEPH BROWN,
RICH'D COTTRELL.

AT A VESTRY, held at Richmond Town, on Tuefday, the 8th day of December, 1772, for laying the Parifh Levy.

Prefent.

The Rev'd Miles Selden, Rich'd Randolph, Samuel Duval, Jos. Lewis, Rich'd Adams, Daniel Price, George Cox and Turner Southall, Veftrymen.

The Parifh,	*Dr.*
	lbs. Tob'o.
To the Rev'd Mr. Selden, his Annual Sall'y,	17,150
To Wm. Street, Clk D. Run Church,	1,789

To Jas. Sharp, do. Curl's,	1,789
To John Bryan, do. Richmond,	1,789
To Jos. Ellis, do. Deep Run,	536
To Fortu. Sydnor, Clk Veftry,	536
To Ch. W'dns, for Church Elements,	536
To Thomas Alley,	500
To Ch. W'dns, for Matt. Bridgman,	300
To do., for Margaret Childers,	250
To do., John Weft,	500
To do., for John Grimftead for Wife,	700
To do., for Molly Hogg and children,	700
To do., for Nath'l Bridgwater,	500
To do., for Aaron Freeman's Wife,	1,000
To do., Henry Britain,	500
To do., for Capt. McBurnet,	1,000
To do., for Benja. Goode,	1,000
To Mary Franklin,	500
To Mary Swinton,	600
To Richard Moore,	1,000
To John Enroughty, for felf and fon,	600
To John Orange,	600
To John Childers and wife,	1,000
To Matthew Jordan,	300
To Jane Morris,	1,000
To Efther Stedman,	300
To John Ragland, for Rachel Burton, orphan of Benjamin Burton,	500
To Richard Cottrell, for Pridgeon Waddell, as per Acco. £17, 4, 8½,	500
To Sufa. Parfons, for Henry Britains and Pridgeon Waddels, as per Acco., £7, 4, 6,	
To Geo. Scherrer, for Burying a man that was drown'd, per Acco., £1, 5, 0,	
John Gordon, Exempted paying Levy,	
To Doct. P. Strachan, per Acco., £6, 2, 3,	
To John Myers, per Acco., £3, 0, 0,	
To Mary Thomfon,	500
To Ch. W'ds, for Shad. Vaughan, Alt. Simpfon, a bastard child of A. Weft,	300

To Jas. Sharp, D. Sheriff, for Infolv'ts, per Acco.,	300
To William Burton, do., for do.,	150
To Com's, for collecting,	3,329
To Depofitam, in Collectors Hands,	12,796
	55,660

Cr.

By 2,420 Tiths, @ 23 ℔. per Poll,	55,660

Ord'd, Ch. W'dns bring Suit Ag't Mr. Sam'l Duval on his Agreem't for Bricking in the Lands belonging to Richmond Church, he having failed to do the fame accd'g to f'd Agreem't.

It is the Opinion of the Veftry that an addition of Forty feet in Length and the fame Width as the preft. Church at Richmond, be built to it, at the North fide, with Gallery on both fides, and one end with proper windows above and below; and Ordered that the Ch. W'dns Lett to the Loweft Bidder the faid addition.

Mr. Thos. Watkins[29] and Mr. William Randolph[30] are chofen Veftrymen in the room of Wm. Lewis and Bowler Cocke, dec'd.

Daniel Price and Turner Southall are appointed Ch. W'dns for the enfuing year.

Nath'l Wilkinfon, Sheriff, is appointed Collector of this levy, and that he give Bond to the Ch. Wd'ns for Collecting of fame.

TURNER SOUTHALL,
DANIEL PRICE.

AT A VESTRY, held at Richmond, on Fryday, the 17th Day of December, 1773, for laying the Parifh Levy.

Prefent.

The Rev'd Mr. Selden, Sam'l Duval, Jofeph Lewis, Daniel Price, George Cox, Turner Southall, Nath'l Wilkinfon and Thomas Watkins.

Dr. *Henrico Parifh.*

	Lbs. Tobo.	£	S	D.
To Rev'd Mr. Selden, his Annual Salary,	17,150	125	1	0
To Wm. Street, Clk Deep Run Church,	1,789	13	0	10
To Jas. Sharp, do., at Curl's,	1,789	13	0	10
To a Salary to be paid a clk Richmond Church, hereafter to be app'd, and to remain in the Church Wardens hands till fuch appointment,	1,789	13	0	10
To R'd Trueman, clk Boar Swamp Church,[31]	500	3	12	11
To the Sexton of Curl's Church,	536	3	15	07
To R'd Williams, Sexton of the Town Church, and a power granted the Ch. W'dns to difplace him if they think fit,	536	3	13	07
To Jos. Freeman, who is App'd Sexton of Deep Run Church, in the room of Jos. Ellis,	536	3	15	07
To Fortu. Sydnor, clk Veftry,	500	3	12	11
To the Ch. Wardens, for Ch. El'mnts,	300	2	3	09
To Thomas Alley,	500	3	12	11
To Ch. Wardens, for Matt. Bridgman,	700	5	2	01
To do., per Margaret Childrefs,	1,000	7	5	10
To do., per John Weft and Daughter,	1,000	7	5	10
To John Grimftead, for his Wife,	500	3	22	11
To do., for Molly Hogg and children,	700	5	2	01
To do., for Nath'l Bridgwater,	800	5	16	08
To do., Catharine McBurnet,	500	3	12	11
To do., for Ben. Goode,	600	4	7	06
To do., for Mary Frankling,	1,000	7	5	10
To Mary Swinton,	600	4	7	06
To Rich'd Moore,	800	5	16	08
To John Enroughty, for felf and fon,	1,000	7	5	10
To John Orange, in the Ch. Wardens,	1,000	7	5	10
To Martha Jordan,	300	2	3	9
To Jane Morris,	500	3	12	11

To John Ragland, for Rachel Burton, orphan of Ben Burton,	500	3	12	11
To Sufa, Clarke,	200	2	2	01
To Matthew Bridgman, in the Ch. Wardens hands, for keep'g Michael Culling, Sen.,	500	3	12	11
To. B. Price, for keeping Jas. Cullington,	600	4	7	06
To Elvia. Clarke,	600	4	7	06
To Mary Thompfon,	300	2	3	09
To Sufa. Clark, for keeping Waddell Brittain,		36	6	09
To Robert Spears, for Repairs done to Boar Swamp Church,		1	15	00
To Sam'l Robinfon, for keeping John Thompfon,		8	0	00
To Jofeph Ellis, for Steps to D. R. Church,			5	00
To Clark and Halland,		3	9	07
To Jno. Redcrofs,		1	0	00
To Thomas Watkins, for Elv'a Baker,	300	3	2	09
		345	12	15
To the Sheriff, for collect'g, £551, 3, 1,		33	8	06
		379	0	11
To a Depofit'm, to remain in the hands of the Church Wardens to pay Contingent Charges,		178	2	02
	£557	3	3	01

Cr.

By 2,547 Tythes at 30 ℔s. tob'o or 4, 4½ per Poll, at the option of the payer,	£557	3	01

Peter Winfton,[32] Gent., is app'd Collector of this Levy and ord'd he give Bond and Sec'y to the Church Wardens for that purpofe, and it is further Ordered, that he purchafe a

ALMS BASIN AND COMMUNION SERVICE.

fuff'ct quantity of Tobacco to difcharge the Salary of the Rev'd Mr. Selden.

Daniel Price and Turner Southall, Gent., Church Wardens, returned an Account with the parifh, the ball'ce wherof due to the f'd Parifh is, £74, 3, 1¼. Ord., The Clk record the f'd Acc't, and in future every account of the like nature, for which the Veftry will make an allowance.

Ord., That Church Wardens pay Geo. Rowland £24, 0, 0, and that Richard Adams and Geo. Cox pay him the further fum of £75, 0, 0, if fo much in their hands, in part for the Brick Wall he is about to raife round the town Church.

Dan'l Price and Nath'l Wilkinfon are app'd Church Wardens for the Enfuing Year.

DANIEL PRICE,
NAT. WILKINSON.

Dr. Henrico Parifh in Acco. with Daniel Price and Turner Southall.

1772.					
Feb. 7,	To Cafh p'd for Neceffarys for Mary Bol'g,			5	9
	To Cafh p'd for a Bible and Prayer Book for Boar Swamp Meeting Houfe,		4	10	0
	To Cafh p'd for the Poft, for bringing the Books,			5	0
	To Cafh p'd the Printer, for Advertizing the Building—the Church,			7	0
	To Bufhels of Corn for Matt Bridgeman,			5	7
	To the Depofitam in tob'o,	12,796 lbs.			
	To Henry Britton,	1,000			
		13,796			
	To 2 pr. ct. on 11,102 lbs. Tob'o, at 18 per,		1	19	11¼
	To 10 Cafks, at 30 lbs. Tob'o each, 300 at 18 per,		2	14	0

	To Priz'g 10 Hhds. Tob'o, at 2-6,	1	5	0
Aug'ft 21,	To 2 Bufh'ls Corn, for Matt Bridgman,		2	6
	To 1 Pr. of Shoes, of John McKnead, for H. Britton,		6	1
Sept. 6,	To Cafh p'd Dr. Strachan, his Acco.,	6	2	3
Oct. 4,	To Cafh p'd Mrs. Parfons, ditto,	7	4	6
	To 7 Yds. Linen, of W. Mitchel, for H. Britton,		15	10½
	To 1 oz. Thread, for do.,			7½
	To 1 ℔. Coffee, for Matt Brigman,		1	6
	To 2 ℔. Bro. Sugar, for Ditto,		1	3
28,	To 1¼ ℔. bro. thr'd, 5 Ells Rolls, 4-7 qts, Rum, for Henry Britton,		8	1
	To Cafh p'd Rich'd Cottrell, his Acco.,	17	4	8½
	To do., Jno. Sherrer,	1	5	
	To do., Jno. Myers,	3	0	0
	To Ball per Contra,	74	3	2¼
		£122	7	2

Dr. *Henrico Parifh in acco. with D'l Price and T. Southall,*

Cr.

1773.				
	By 4 Hhds. Tob'o, fold Neil Campbell, 4,349 ℔s. @ per,	39	2	9¾
	By 6 Ditto, fold Richard Harmon, 4,753, @ 18 per,	60	15	4½
	By Tob'o fold the Sheriff on the Notes, 2,694, @ 2 d.,	22	9	0
		£122	7	2
	By Ballance due the Parifh,	£74	3	1¼

Truly Recorded.
Teste,

FORTU. SYDNOR, *C. V.*

Dr. Henrico Parish in Acco. with
Turner Southall and Daniel Price, Ch. Wdn's.

1773.	
Dec. 18, To Cafh p'd George Rowland,	24 0 0
1774.	
Sept. 24, To Cafh p'd Smith Blakey,	50 0 0
To Ball'ce due per Contra,	3 1¾
	£74 3 1¾

Cr.

1773.	
Nov. By Ball'ce Rendered this date,	£74 3 1¾

Errors Excepted,

TURNER SOUTHALL.

Teft,

FORTU. SYDNOR,
C. V.

A.

B.

C.

Ann Cocke, the daughter of Bowler Cocke and Sarah his wife, was born at Bowler's Farm, on Rappahannock river, the Eighteenth day of June, MDCCXX.

Sufanna Cocke, daughter to the faid Bowler and Sarah, was born at Bremo, the Sixth day of November, MDCCXII, and died the October following.

Tabitha Cocke, was born the twenty-fifth of September, MDCCXXIV.

Bowler Cocke, was born the Eleventh Day of March, MDCCXXVI.

Sarah Cocke was born the Sixth day of February, MDCCXXVIII.

Eliza. Cocke was born the fifteenth day of May, MDCCXXXI.

Richard Cocke was born the Seventh day of March, MDCCXXXIII, and lived but twenty-five days.

Charles Cocke was born the Ninth day of September, MDCCXXXV, and died the Fourth Day of Auguft, MDCCXXXIX.

D.

E.

F.

G.

H.

I.

K.

Francis Kemp, Son of Alexander Kemp and Matilda his wife was (*born*) ye 13 day of October, 1735.

L.

Ann Lunfford, Daughter of Hannah Lunfford, mulatto, was born Sept'r 13, 1731.

Elizabeth Lunfford, daughter of faid Hannah, was Born July ye 10 Day, 1732.

William Lunfford, Son of faid Hannah, was born March ye V day, 1735.

John Lunfford, Son of faid Hannah, was born Seut'r ye 19 Day, 1737.

Mary Lunfford, Daughter of faid Hannah, was born March 1 Day, 1739.

Entered, October ye 14, 1740.

Delivered me by Capt. John Redford.

SACK BREWER,
Clk C Vefy.

Catherine Lorton, Daughter of Robert Lorton and Lucretia his wife, was born the 12th March, 1737-8.

Ann Lorton, Daughter of the faid Robert Lorton and Lucretia his Wife, was born Auguft 15th, 1740.

Thomas Lorton was born July the 14th, 1746.

Robert Lorton was born January 11th, 1749.

M.

Arthur Mofby was killed by a fall from his Horfe ye 4th day of October, Anno Dom. 1736.

Ann Middleton, Daughter of John Middleton and Judith his Wife, was born ye 12 Day of October, Anno Dom. MDCCXXXVII.

N.

O.

P.

Elizabeth Poval, Daughter of Robert Povall and Judith his wife, was born in December, Anno 1729.

Robert Povall, Son of the Above faid Robert and Judith, was born ye 3rd Day of July, Anno 1732.

R.

Sarah, the Wife of Jno. Rees, who lately Arrived here in the Snow Phœnax, from London, departed this life the thirtieth day of Aug'ft, Anno 1739.

S.

Richard Sharp, Son of Henry Sharp and Mary his wife, was born ye 1 day of January, 1735.

Mary, the Daughter of Henry Sharp and Mary his wife, was born the laft day of September, 1739.

Henry, the Son of do., was born ye 27 day of March, 1734.

Ann the Daughter of do., was born ye 10th day of June, 1741.

T.

Michael Taylor, departed this life ye 11 Day of January, Anno 1735.

U.

V.

W.

Y.

DEATHS REGISTERED.

Edmund Liptrot, departed this life December ye 12, 1735.

Benjamin Hobfon, departed this life Decemb'r ye 29, 1735.

Mrs. Mary Randolph,[33] departed this life Decemb'r ye 29, 1735.

No Perfon fhall be Admitted a Veftryman or Church Warden untill he has taken the Oaths and fubfcribed to be conformable to the Doctrines and Difcipline of the Church of England, as enjoined by the Statiftics of 1 W. and M.

I do fincerely promife and fwear that I will be faithful and bear true allegiance to his Majefty King George So help me God.

I do fwear that I do, from my heart, abhor, deteft and adjure as impious and heretical, that Damnable Doctrine and profition, that Princes excommunicated by the Pope, or any authority of the See of Rome, may be Depofed by their fubjects or any other whatfoever. And I do declare, that no foreign Prince, perfon, prelate, State or Potentate, hath or Ought to have any Jurifdition, power, Superiority, pre-eminent or Authority, Ecclefiaftical or Spiritual, within this Realm. So help me God.

THE DECLARATION.

I, do declare that I do believe that there is not any Transfubftantiation in the Sacrament of the Lord's Supper, or in his Elements of Bread and Wine at or After the Confecration thereof, by any perfon whatfoever.

JOHN COLES,
WM. FINNEY,
WM. LEWIS.

Feb. 8th, JOHN ELLIS.
1749. BOWLER COCKE, jun'r.

THE OATH OF A CHURCH WARDEN.

You fhall Execute the Office of a Church Warden in the Parifh where you are Chofen for the enfuing year, According to your Skill and Difcretion in his Majes. Laws, Ecclesiastical, now in force.

So help you God.

NOTES.

By Dr. R. A. Brock.

Note 1. *Curls Church.*—Though the orthography *Curls* appears to have quite generally obtained at the period of the text, and is, we are led to conclude, the only usage at the present time, it is obviously incorrect; the derivation being undoubtedly from the Virginia family name of *Curle,* to members of which, grants of land, extending over a period of one hundred years, may be found recorded in the books of the State Land Registry Office. A prominent representative of the family was the patriot Wilson Roscow Curle, of the Revolutionary era.

The church was situated on the north side of James river, distant some eight or nine mile below the city of Richmond. Bishop Meade terms it "the Four Mile Creek, or Curls Church," and erroneously, [as is patent from the text,] gives the time of its erection as 1748. He bases his conclusion upon the following extract from a letter bearing date that year, from Richard Randolph of Curls, to his son Richard: "Pray assist Wilkinson all you can in getting the church finished, and get the shells that will be wanted carted before the roads get bad. The joiner can inform you what shells I have at the Falls; if more are wanted you must get them."*

*Old Churches and Families of Va., vol. 1, p. 138.

The Randolphs frequently undertook building. It is said that William Randolph, of Turkey Island, the first of the name in the Colony of Virginia, laid the foundations of the wealth and importance of his family, from the profits acquired in "building barns."† One account states that he landed in the Colony of Virginia with a "broad-axe upon his shoulder."‡ Col. Richard Randolph contracted, in 1739, to build the church at Richmond, agreeing to complete it by the 10th of June, 1741. It is not likely that it was so late as 1748 in being finished. At a meeting of the parish vestry, held October the 2d, 1742, a meeting of the Vestry was agreed upon, to be held at Curls Church in November following, to treat with undertakers for building a Chapel at Deep Run, and an appropriation was made towards the same of 10,000 lbs. of tobacco. This was, in all probability, the Church mentioned in the letter above quoted from. In May, 1826, Dr. John Adams presented to the Vestry of St. John's Church, Richmond, the baptismal font which had been used at Curls Church.§ It is of white marble, and is in perfect preservation. Curls Church was demolished within the past twenty years.

NOTE 2. *Col. Richard Randolph of Curls,* the son of Wm. Randoph of Turkey Island, was the grandfather of that meteoric, though most erratic genius, John Randolph of Roanoke. He married Jane, the daughter of John Bolling of Cobbs, who was the great-grandson of Pocahontas, his mother being Jane, the daughter of Thomas Rolph, or Rolfe, hence

†Grigsby's Va. Convention of 1776, p. 77. Campbell's Va., p. 424.
‡Neill's Va. Papers.
§Ms. Vestry Book of St. John's Church. [Period commencing 1785.]

the royal aboriginal descent so much vaunted by these families. Richard Randolph was a member of the House of Burgesses from Henrico, in 1740, and succeeded his brother William as Treasurer of the Colony. He died in England, December 17th, 1748, in the 58th year of his age. His widow died March 4th, 1766, aged 62 years.

Mss. Mem. Book of John Randolph of Roanoke.

NOTE 3. *Thomas Jefferson.*—The ancestors of the Jefferson family in Virginia are said to have emigrated from near Mount Snowden, in Wales. They were among the first settlers of the Colony. The name, Jefferson, appears as the representative from Fleur de Hundred, in the Colonial Assembly, which, by order of Governor Yeardly, was convened in the choir of the Church at Jamestown, on the 30th of July, 1619. This was the first legislative body of Europeans, [so far as our historical records exhibit,] that ever assembled in the New World. The first Jefferson of whom any definite accounts are preserved, was Thomas Jefferson, who resided at Osborne's, on James River, in the now county of Chesterfield, which was formed from Henrico in 1748. He occupied a respectable social station, and was possessed of a competency. His children were three in number—sons: Thomas, of the text, [who died in the year 1731, his brother Peter being his executor,] Field and Peter, the father of President Jefferson, who was born February, 1708, and married, in 1738, Jane, the daughter of Isham Randolph, of Dungeress, in Goochland county. Peter Jefferson, though he enjoyed but few advantages of early education, was a man of vigorous intellect. Having adopted the profession of a surveyor, by continuous application he had made himself so proficient in his calling, that he was chosen, in connection with Joshua Fry, Professor of Mathematics in William and Mary College, to continue the boundary line between Virginia and North Carolina, and afterwards assisted Mr. Fry in preparing a map of the Colony of Virginia. Peter Jefferson was one of the first settlers, [about the year 1737,] of that portion of the county of Goochland which now forms that of Albemarle —the latter being formed in 1744. Goochland itself was carved from Henrico, in 1727. Peter Jefferson was a man of extraordinary physical strength; he could "head up," that is raise from their sides to an upright position, at once, two hogsheads of tobacco weighing near a thousand pounds each. He died in 1757, leaving a widow, [who survived until 1776,] with six daughters and two sons, of whom Thomas, then fourteen years of age, was the elder.

Randall's Jefferson, vol. 1, pp. 5, 6. Campbtll's Va., p. 604, and the text.

NOTE 4. *Parish Levies.*—By enactment, the sheriffs of the county, or an appointment of one of their number by respective parish vestries, was required to collect the public and parish levies, giving bond and security for the faithful performance of his duties. The assessments were made for loose tobacco, and for every hundred pounds paid in hogshead, an allowance of eight per cent. was made for the hogshead or "cask." The collector was empowered to distrain for failure or delay in payment. Each parish was required to support its own paupers, and the inhabitants of one parish were forbidden, under a penalty, to entertain, hire or employ any tithable person from another parish, unless he or she could produce a receipt from the collector of the parish from whence removing, for the taxes for the preceding year. All vagrants were adjudged "rogues and vagabonds," and were bound out for one year, if a hirer could be found. But if of such evil repute that no one would receive them, the County Court was empowered to order them "thirty-nine lashes on the bare back, well laid on, at the whipping-post, and then discharged." They were liable, however, to re-arrest and repeated punishment. Vagrants and paupers were authorized to be returned to the parishes of which they had last been resident. The Church Wardens were empowered to bind out, to the age of maturity, the children of such persons as were deemed incapable of supporting or bringing them up in "honest courses."

Hening's Statutes, vol. III, p. 264; *vol. VI, pp.* 29, 32.

NOTE 5. *Joseph Mayo* emigrated from the Island of Barbadoes, to Virginia, about the year 1727.* He was a merchant, and from the text, appears to have also followed surveying. His residence was Powhatan, the location of which is well authenticated as a residence of the aboriginal potentate of this name.† It is about a half mile below Richmond, and lies "to the south of the road which runs parallel with the river, and on a verge of the second bank, or upper level of alluvium, some forty feet above the lower. The ground falls abruptly on the front or river side, and more gradually on the other quarters. On the east, the deep channel of a brook separates it from the most commanding point of the upland." Immediately on the selection of

---

*Bishop Meade's Old Churches and Families, vol. II, p. 39.

†Mss. Deed Book of Wm. Byrd of Westover, p. 93.

Jamestown for the seat of the Colony, "Newport, Smith and twentie others were sent to discover the head of the river. By divers small habitations they passed, in six days they arrived at a town called Powhatan, consisting of some twelve houses, pleasantly seated on a hill; before it three fertile isles; about it many of their corne-fields; the place is very pleasant, and strong by nature—of this place the prince is called Powhatan, and the people Powhatans—to this place the river is navigable; but higher, within a myle, by reason of the Rockes and Isles, there is not passage for a small Boat; this they call the Falles."‡ "A granite boulder, about a ton in weight, is pointed out as 'Powhatan's Tombstone,'" but there is no evidence justifying the designation. It bears many traces of rude carving. A row of symmetrical holes, an inch or more deep, runs along the top. On the sloping side, are graven marks of the shape of a child's and an adult's foot, a horse-shoe, and others less distinguishable. These are obviously of far greater age than other cuttings on the same surface, which are dated 1741, and which give in two or three places, the initial M., of the family in possession: Mayo."§ In a narrative of "Capt. Newport's discoveries, Virginia," May 21st, 1607, Powhatan is thus described: "We came to the second inlet described in the ryver; over against on Popham syde, in the habitatyon of the greate Kyng Pawatah [one of the early modes of spelling Powhatan,] which I call Pawatah's Tower. It is scituat upon a highe hill by the water syde; a playne between it and the

‡Smith Hist. of Va., Richmond, Reprint, 1819, vol. I, pp. 151-2.

§Loungings in the Footprints of the Pioneers W. C. Bruce, Harper's Mag., May, 1859.

water, twelve score over, whereon he sowes his wheate, beane, peaze, tobacco, pompions, gowrds, hempe, flaxe, &c.; and were any art used to the naturall state of this place it would be a goodly habitatyon."‖ The brother of Joseph Mayo, Major William Mayo, is supposed to have settled in the Colony about the same time. He accompanied, as one of the surveyors, in the years 1728-9, the commission which ran the dividing line between Virginia and North Carolina, so racily chronicled in the Westover Mss. He also, in 1737, laid off for Col. William Byrd, [the second of the name,] the town of Richmond. The brothers were the ancestors of the present very respectable family of Mayo in Virginia. Col. Wm. Mayo, Jr., of Pawhatan, served in the State line during the revolution, and was a member of the House of Delegates in 1780.

The late Hon. Joseph Mayo, for a long series of years Mayor of Richmond, a worthy representative of this family, compiled, we have been informed, a genealogy which connected with the Mayos of England. It is to be hoped that it will be made public; the editor craves the privilege of copying.

NOTE 6. *Processioning.*—By Statute, every fourth year, between the last day of September and the last day of March following, the bounds of every person's land were required to be processioned, or "gone round," and the land-marks renewed. Such marks being made by chopping the trees. The parishes were divided into precincts, and free-holders, at least two to every precinct, appointed to perform such duty.

‖Archeologia, Americana, Trans. and Coll. Am. Ant. Soc., vol. IV, p. 44.

They were required to make a return, in writing, to the parish vestry of the result of their action. It was "*Provided always,* That the processioning and settling the bounds of any lands belonging to any person being within the age of one and twenty years, feme covert, *non compos mentis,* imprisoned or out of the Colony, shall not be conclusive to such person until after the expiration of six years from and after the said severall capacitys shall be removed and determined."

Hening's Statutes, vol. III, pp. 327-8.

NOTE 7. *Field Jefferson,* the brother of Thomas and Peter Jefferson, who died young and unmarried.

NOTE 8. *William Randolph* was the second of the name, of Turkey Island, where he is buried. He married Eliza Beverley, of Gloucester county. Had issue: Beverly, of Turkey Island; Peter, of Chatsworth, and William, of Wilton. The following is the inscription upon his monument:

Here lieth the Honorable
William Randolph, Esquire, Eldest Son
of Colo. William Randolph, of this place,
and of Mary, his wife,
who was of the antient and eminent family
of the Ishams, of Northamptonshire.
Having been introduced early into Business,
and passed thro' many of the inferior offices of Government,
with great reputation & eminent capacity,
He was at last,
By his Majesty's happy choice,
and the universal approbation of his country,
advanced to the Council.
His experience in Men & Business,
The native gravity & dignity
of his Person & Behaviour,
his attachments to the Interests of his Country,

knowledge of the laws in general,
and of the laws and Constitution
of this Colony in particular,
his Integrity above all calumny or suspicion,
the acuteness of his parts,
and the extensiveness of his genius,
Together with that solidity of Sense and judgment
which were predominant in all he said or did,
Rendered him not only equal,
but an ornament to the high office he bore,
and made him universally lament'd
as a most able & impartial Judge,
and an upright magistrate
in all other respects.
Neither was he less conspicuous
for a certain majestic plainness
of Sense and Honour, which carried him
through all parts of private life
with equal dignity and reputation,
and deservedly obtained him the character
of a just and good man
in all the several duties & relations of Life.

Natus, } Nov., 1681.
Mortuus, } Oct. 19, 1742.

The following in relation to the origin of the designation, *Turkey Island,* we hope may not be thought uninteresting. It is extracted from a quaint tract: "A RELATYON OF THE DISCOVERY OF OUR RIVER (JAMES) FROM JAMES FORKE INTO THE MAINE; MADE BY CAPT. CHRISTOPHER NEWPORT, AND SINCERELY WRITTEN AND OBSERVED BY A GENTLEMAN OF THE COLONY." (State paper office America and the West Indies.) The author of which has recently been determined, upon proofs adduced by Prof. William Green, LL. D., Richmond, Va., to have been Capt. Gabriel Archer. On

Thursday, May 21st, 1607, (Campbell, Hist. of Va., gives the date as June 4th,) Capt. Christopher Newport "having fitted our shallop with provision"—"tooke five gentlemen, four maryners, and fourteen saylors; (the names are all given, Smith mentions only himself, Newport and twentie others,) with whom he proceeded, with a perfect resolutyon not to returne; but either to find the head of this ryver, the laake mentyoned by others heretofore, the sea againe, the mountynes Apalatsi, (Appalachian, modern,) or some issue." Having narrated a voyage of thirteen miles, the account proceeds as follows: "May 22, Friday. Omitting no tyme, we passed up some sixteen myle further." [By recent measurement, the distance from City Point, near which is Turkey Island, to Newport News, (properly and originally Newport Nuce,) has been ascertained to be thirty miles, and to Jamestown, forty miles,] where wee found an ilet, on which were many turkeys, and greate store of young byrdes like black birdes; whereof we took dyvers, which we brake our fast with all," "the ryver skants of his breadth two mile before we come to the ilet mentyoned, (which I call Turkey Ile.")

Archeologia Americana—Trans. Am. Ant. Soc., Vol. IV. pp. 41-2.

Note 9. *John Bolling,* of Cobbs, the son of Robert Bolling, (son of John and Mary Bolling, of Bolling Hall, who lived in the parish of All-halloway, or Allhallows, Barkin Parish, Town street, London, the first of the name who settled in Va.," born Dec. 26th, 1646, arrived in Va. Oct. 2d, 1660,) and Jane Rolfe, the grand-daughter of Pocahontas, was born Jan. 27th, 1676, and died April 10th, 1729. He devoted himself to commence and amassed a large fortune.[*] His daughter Jane, married the first Richard Randolph of Curles.

Mr. John Bolling, Surveyor, is mentioned in 1704.[†]

NOTE 10. *The Rev. James Keith.*—The Rev. Mr. Keith removed to Maryland in 1735[‡]—doubtless him of the text. The name is a prominent one now, not only in that State, but also in Pennsylvania and Virginia.

NOTE 11. *The Rev. David Mossom* was born in London, Mch. 25th, 1690, and died Jan. 4th, 1767. He was the Rector of St. Peter's Church, New Kent Co., Va., for a period of forty years preceding his death. A beautiful marble tablet in the wall, on the right hand side of the pulpit, *did* record his virtues. "He officiated at the nuptials of General Washington, at the White House, a few miles from St. Peter's Church."[||] This venerable place of worship was the victim of the vandalism of the Federal troops during the late war, its associations with the memory of the Father of his Country finding no responsive chord in the breasts of those zealous patriots, to stay their vengeful hands. "The Church itself was broken and battered, and rendered wholly unfit for use. The old massive stone font, in which the children of two centuries had been baptized, was broken and scattered in fragments over the floor. The chancel was torn down, the pulpit and desk broken and defaced, and not a sash was left in the windows."[§] The monument to Mr. Mosson was also

*Memois of the Bolling Family, p. 4.
†Papers of the Virginia Church, Steevens, p. 96.
‡Perry's Va. Papers, p. 358.
||Bishop Meade's Old Churches, &c., Vol. I, p. 386; Vol. II, p. 490.
§The Communication in the "Richmond Dispatch" of Feb 6, 1871, over the signature "Senex."

destroyed—nought but fragments remaining. The parishoners lately appealed to the public for contributions to aid them to so far repair the old church, that divine service might be resumed within its hallowed halls.

NOTE 12. *Darby Enroughty.*—The locality, Darbytown, situate a few miles below Richmond, owes its designation to its having been at one time almost exclusively peopled by those bearing the name Darby or Enroughty. It being a remarkable fact that the two names, in common parlance among them, are regarded as synonymous and interchangeable. The first, Darby, obtaining prevalence because of its brevity and easier pronunciation. (It is claimed, and with apparent reason, that the name was originally *Derby,* which among the lower English classes is even now pronounced, as by those simple people.) Those of them, however, who are able to write their names, (in doing so,) generally use that of Enroughty—which name indeed a majority of them affix to legal instruments.

We venture the highly probable conjecture that the individual above was the progentor of this humble, honest and simple family. His neighbors and succeeding generations, with a wayward ruthlessness which is constantly repeating itself in matters of popular designation, adopting the cognomen which least taxed their linguistic skill.

NOTE 13. *Isaac Winston.*—The Winstons of Virginia are said to be descended from the ancient and honorable family of that name in England. Four of the name emigrated from Yorkshire, England, some time previous to the year 1710. Three brothers—Isaac, of the text, William Essex and James, and a cousin, Pleasant Winston. They were of the Society of

Friends, and left England to enjoy freedom of religious opinion.

1. Isaac,[1] resided first in Henrico and afterwards in Hanover County, Va. He married Sarah ———.

They had issue:

2. I. Anthony.[2]

3. II. William.[2]

4. III. Mary[2] m. John Coles.

5. IV. Sarah[2] m. first, Col. John Syme, second, Col. John Henry.

2. Anthony,[2] (*Isaac*,[1]) b. Sept. 29th, 1723; m. Feb. 27th, 1747, Alice, (b. May 21st, 1730,) daughter of James and Alice Taylor, of Caroline Co., Va.

They had issuse:

I. Sarah, b. Feb. 9th, 1748, died unmarried.

6. II. Anthony, b. Nov. 25th, 1750, m. Mch. 11th, 1776, Kezia Jones.

7. III. Alice, b. Mch. 20th, 1753, m. her cousin, Judge Edmund Winston, d. Feb., 1784.

IV. Martha, b. June 3d, 1759, m. Charles Woodson, of Buckingham Co.

6. Anthony[3] (*Anthony*,[2] *Isaac*,[1]) removed to Buckingham County, near the "New Store," in 1771; m. Mch. 11th, 1776, Kesia, (b. Feb. 1760,) daughter of John and Elizabeth (Walker) Jones, from Wales. Anthony Winston was a Member both of the House of Burgesses and the patriot Virginia Convention of 1775, from the County of Buckingham. He was also a Captain in the Army of the Revolution, and a gallant officer. He was the purchaser of Peter Francisco, famous for his feats of valor and strength, whom he released from slavery to allow to enlist in the patriotic army. He was sheriff of Buckingham County for a long series of years. He removed to Davidson Co., Tenn., in the autumn of 1801.

Anthony and Kezia had issue:

I. Anthony, b. Dec. 5th, 1782.

II. John Jones, b. May 31st, 1785.

III. Edmund, b. May, 2d, 1787, died in childhood.

8. IV. William, b. Mch. 24th, 1789, d. 1859.

9. V. AliceTaylor, b. Dec. 21st, 1790, m. John, son of John Pettus, of Fluvania Co., Va. His sister, Mrs. Shelton Burgess, was living May, 1871, in her 80th year, with her son John, near Bremo Bluff, Fluvanna Co.

VI. Joel Walker, b. Dec. 6th, 1792.

VII. Isaac, b. Jan. 22d, 1795.

VIII. Mary Walker, b. Nov. 6th, 1796, m. Jesse Jones

IX. Betsy, b. Sept. 15th, 1798, d. an infant.

X. Edmund, (second of the name,) b. June 15th, 1801, d. since the late war.

XI. Thomas, b. May 3d, 1804, settled in Davidson Co., Tenn.

In 1811 or '12, all of the children of Anthony and Kezia Winston, excepting the two youngest (who remained with their parents in Tennessee,) removed to that locality of Mississippi Territory, which now constitutes Madison County, Alabama.

"In 1813, when the war with the Creek nation commenced, a family council was held in Madison County, to determine which one of the seven brothers, and brothers-in-law should be selected to remain and protect all the families," whilst the other six "went to the war." "Wm. Winston was selected on account of his firmness and prudence to protect the young families." The wives as well as their husbands were in the Council. "John Jones Winston was a

Captain, and his eldest brother, Anthony, a Lieutenant in his company—the other five served in the ranks." General Jackson "was the personal friend of all these young men," and bore cheerful testimony to the gallantry of each.

10. John Anthony Winston,[5] son of (*William*[4] *Anthony,*[3] *Anthony,*[2] *Isaac,*[1]) d. Dec. 22d, 1871. He represented Sumpter Co., Ala., for many years in the General Assembly as Representative or Senator. He was Colonel of the ——— Ala. Regt., Volunteer Infantry, during the Mexican war; for two terms Governor of Alabama; President of the State Senate; Colonel Eighth Alabama Infantry, during the late war, participating in the battles fought on Virginia soil. He was elected United States Senator in 1866, but was not allowed to take his seat. He is described as having possessed an "unbending will" and a vigorous intellect. His style of speech was "bold and incisive." He was never called an orator, but as a debater, he had few, if any, equals in the State. His personal courage was undoubted. He was as he represented his family as being: "very tolerant in matters of religious faith."

11. John Jones Pettus,[5] son of (*John and Alice Taylor,*[4] *Pettus, Anthony Winston,*[3] *Anthony,*[2] *Isaac,*[1]) was educated for the bar, but preferred planting. He was for many years before the late war a Member of the Mississippi Legislature in both of its branches. He was twice Governor of that State.

Edmund Winston Pettus, brother of the preceding, was Solicitor for the State of Alabama for eight years; Judge of the Circuit Court of the State; Major and Lieutenant Colonel 20th Regiment Alabama Infantry, and Brigadier-General Confederate States Army during the late war. He was a gallant and efficient officer, and received the encomiums of his superior officers. He is now a distinguished practitioner of law in Selma, Ala.

12. William Winston,[2] son of (*Isaac*,[1]) was called Langaloo William. "He was a great hunter; had a quarter in Bedford or Albemarle County; spent half the year there hunting deer. He was fond of the Indians, and dressed like them, and was a favorite with them. An amour with the daughter of an Indian Chief, who was engaged to another Chief, involved him in difficulties with the savages. They besieged him in a log fort for a week. He defended himself with the aid of three negroes with rifles. Tom, one of the negroes, stood guard every night; at length the favorite squaw went out and made peace between the belligerents. Langaloo William was a great Indian fighter."* He was endowed with those impassioned powers of natural and all-prevailing oratory, which rendered his nephew, Patrick Henry, the patriot, immortal. Wirt, in his life of the latter, quotes the following anecdote from a correspondent—Wm. Pope: "I have often heard my father, who was intimately acquainted with this William Winston, say, that he was the greatest orator he ever heard—Patrick Henry excepted. That during the last French and Indian war, and soon after Braddock's defeat, when the militia were marched to the frontiers of Virginia against the Indians, this William Winston was a Lieutenant of a company. That the men who were indifferently clothed, without tents, and exposed to the rigor and inclemency of the weather, discovered great aversion to the service, and were anxious and were clamorous to return to their families; when William Winston mounting a stump (the common rostrum of the field orator of Virginia,) and addressed them with keenness of invective, and declaimed with such force of eloquence on liberty and patriotism, that when he concluded, the general cry was 'Let us march on; lead us against the enemy!' and they were now willing, nay anxious, to encounter all those difficulties and dangers which but a few minutes before had almost produced mutiny."

William Winston[2] had issue:

I. Elizabeth, a beauty, m. Peter Fontaine.

---

*Article in the Virginia Standard, 185—.

II. Frances, m. Dr. Walker.

III. Edmund, State Judge, m. first, his cousin, (*Alice,*^{3} *daughter of Anthony,*^{2} *Isaac,*^{1}) died in 1813, in the fifth score year of his age; second, Dolly, (*Dandridge*) the widow of Patrick Henry.

Issue by the first marriage:

I. George m. Dolly, daughter of Patrick Henry.

Issue, five sons who removed to the State of Missouri, and two daughters, one of whom Elvira, m. Dr. Charles Dandridge. "She was a poetical genius, and corresponded with Maria Edgeworth."

II. Edmund m.

III. m. Dr. George Cabell, of Campbell Co.

IV. Alice m. Frederick A. Cabell.

13. Winston,^{4} daughter of (*Judge Edmund*^{3} *and Alice, William,*^{2} *Anthony,*^{2} *Isaac,*^{1}) m. Dr. George Cabell, of Campbell Co.

Had issue:

I. Marian F. m. Landon R. Cabell.

II. Edmund Winston.

III. George K. m. Eliza V. ———.

IV. John B. m. Martha B. ———.

V. William L. m. Eliza ———.

VI. Paulina J. Cabell m. Alexander S. Henry.

VII. Alice Winston m. Walter C. Carrington.

Alice,^{4} daughter of Judge Edmund^{3} and Alice^{3} Winston, m. Frederick A. Cabell. Issue:

I. m. Dr. John Horsley.

II. m. John W. Mosby, uncle of Col. John S. Mosby, Partisan during the late war.

III. Frederick M. m. Coleman.

IV. Edmund Winston m. Lucy Galt.

V. Clifford, M. D., m. Anthony.

VI. Lewis Warrington m. Perkins.

5. Sarah Winston^{2} (*Isaac*^{1}) m. first, Colonel John Syme, Member H. of Burgesses, and of the Virginia Convention of

1775. Col. in the Rev. Issue: Sarah[3] m. Samuel Jordan Cabell, Lieutenant-Colonel Revolution M. O. C. 1795. 1803. Sarah Syme[2] m. second, Col. John Henry, H. of Burgesses, prepared a map of Virginia. Issue:

I. Colonel William, Member of Virginia Assembly, from Fluvanna Co.

II. Patrick (the orator) m. Dolly Dandridge.

III. Lucy m. Valentine Wood.

IV. Jane m. Colonel Samuel Meredith, of Hanover Co.

14. Geddes,[2] son of (*William Essex Winston,*[1]) died June 9th, 1784, and is buried in St. John's Church yard, Richmond. His wife also lies there.

They had issue:

I. Rebecca m. Dr. Wm. Radford.

II. Mary m. Rev. John D. Blair.

III. Samuel Jordan d. unmarried.

IV. Margaret m. Dr. John Adams.

V. Julia m. Dr. John Shore.

VI. Sarah m. Thomas Rutherfoord, of Richmond; enterprising and wealthy merchant and miller, who owned lots in every quarter of the city, which he had purchased during the period of real estate fever which prevailed directly after the war of 1812.

I. Colonel John, Lieutenant-Governor and Acting Governor of Virginia, 1841, d. 1870; m. Emily Ann Coles, who died August 26th, 1871. Issue: John Coles—House of Delegates, from Goochland County, for several years; Emily Ann m. January 24th, 1853, Patrick Henry, son of Philip Aylett—of King William County, a grand-son of Patrick Henry—who lost his life by the calamity of the falling of the floor in the Richmond Capitol, April 27th, 1870.

II. William.

III. Samuel Jordan.

IV. Alexander.

V. Thomas m. first, Josephine Sims; second, Sarah, daughter of Spotswood Wingfield.

VI. Gustavus.

VII. Jane m. Hodijah Meade.
VIII. Sarah m. Wm. B. Randolph, of Chatsworth.
IX. Martha m. Garland Tinsley, of Hanover Co.

15. Dr. John and Margaret (Winston) Adams,[3] (*Geddes,*[2] *William Essex*[1]) had issue:

I. Mary m. Dr. John Minge.

II. Eliza m. John Heron.

III. Margaret m. first, Charles Pickett, second, Colonel George Mayo Carrington, of Richmond.

IV. Martha m. Burwell Moseley, of Norfolk.
V. Louisa m. Dr. Richard A. Carrington.
VI. Elvira m. David Minge.
VII. Richard m. Carter Harrison.
VIII. John m. ———.

4. Mary[2] (*Isaac*[1]) m. Major John Coles, a native of Ireland. He was an early settler of Richmond, where he was engaged in merchandizing. A small frame building recently demolished, (1871) situated on Twenty-second, between Broad and Marshall streets, was pointed out as having been his residence. Many of the timbers, though more than a century old, were in a perfect state of preservation. Major John Coles was buried beneath the old Church at Richmond, the floors of which being removed in 1857, to replace the joists which were in a decayed condition, a metallic plate, bearing his name, was found. It was, however, so much corroded that it fell to pieces.

John and Mary Coles had issue: Four sons and five daughters, of whom—

I. Walter m. Lightfoot, of Sandy Point. Issue: Mildred m. Judge Paul Carrington, the younger.

II. John settled in Albemarle, m. Rebecca, daughter of Henry Tucker. Issue:

I. Mary m. Carter, of Redlands.
II. Rebecca m. John Singleton, of S. C.
III.   m. Hon. Andrew Stevenson.
IV. Elizabeth.
V. Walter.

VI. Edward. First Governor of Illinois, m. first, Lightfoot. Issue: Isaac Coles.

VII. Emily Ann m. Col. John Rutherfoord.

VIII. Tucker.

IX. John.

X. Colonel Isaac m. Catharine Thompson, of New York, a sister of whom married Elbridge Gerry in 1790.

Colonel Isaac and Catharine (*Thompson*) Coles had issue:

I. Walter.
II. Thompson.
III. John.
IV. Robert.
V. Jacob.
VI. Catharine m. Baldwin, son of Philip Payne.
VII. Mary m. James M. Whittle.

The late George Winston, of Richmond, is supposed to have been a descendant of Pleasant Winston, one of the original emigrants—the connecting links cannot, however, be stated by his family.

His children were:

I. James.
II. Pleasants, now residing in Missouri. (He makes claim to a portion of the Chimborazo property of Richmond, which was the site of a Confederate Hospital during the late war.)
III. Virginia J. m. W. F. Butler; d. Nov. 22d, 1872, in her 57th year.

The descendants of James Winston[1] in Hanover, Caroline, Louisa, and Goochland Counties, have long filled offices of local trust, clerks, sheriffs, &c. Mr. Wm. Winston was Lieutenant and Adjutant of Lee's Legion of Cavalry during the Revolution.

The names of John and Benjamin Winston are among the

list of officers pensioned by the State of Virginia for service during the Revolution.

"Joseph Winston, born in Virginia, 1746; d. near Germantown, N. C., 1814. He joined a company of rangers in 1760; was twice wounded in an Indian fight on the Greenbrier; was pensioned by the Legislature for his gallantry; removed to Stokes Sounty, N. C., 1766; was its representative 1775-6, and was appointed a Major; was in several fights victorious, and for his bravery at King's Mountain, where he commanded the right wing, had a sword voted him by the Legislature. Commissioner to Cherokee Indians, with whom a treaty was made in 1777; first Senator from Stokes County, in 1791; and Member of Legislature repeatedly until 1812; M. C. 1793-5 and 1803-7. His son, General Joseph, d. in Platte County, Mo., Mch. 24th, 1810, aged 52. He filled an important position in Stokes County, N. C.; served in the war 1812; was for many years in the State Legislature, and was a Major-General of Militia.—Drake's Dic. Am. Biog.

We take this occasion to express our indebtedness for valuable information embodied in the preceding note, which was rendered us with a prompt heartiness, by the late Hon. John Anthony Winston, of Mobile, and General Edmund Winston Pettus, of Selma, Ala.; whose action is the more highly appreciated, because they were the sole representatives of the Winston Family, from whom we received any manner of assistance—the remainder of our *many* applications having been entirely neglected, or met with unpardonable rudeness.

Our office may have been an unimportant one; it has surely been as thankless as it has been gratuitous.

NOTE 14. *The Reverend Wm. Stith* was the son of William Stith and Mary, the daughter of William Randolph, of Turkey Island.

The issue of William and Mary Stith, was:

I. William, b. 1789; m. Judith, daughter of Thomas Randolph, of Tuckahoe; d. 1755. Issue: Mary, died unmarried.
II. John, of Charles City County, Va.
III. Mary m. Commissary William Dawson, of William and Mary College, Va.

Issue:

A son who m. Johnson, of North Carolina, whose son, William Johnson Dawson, was a Member of Congress 1793-5, from N. C.*

"On the death of her husband, Mrs. Stith, at the instance of her brother, Sir John Randolph, removed to Williamsburg, and placed her son (William) in the grammar-school attached to the College of William and Mary, where he pursued his academic studies, and graduated. His theological studies were completed in England, where he was ordained a Minister of the Episcopal Church. On his return to Virginia, in the year 1731, he was elected Master of the Grammar-school in the College, and Chaplain to the House of Burgesses."† On the 16th of July, 1736, he was installed as Rector of Henrico Parish. At the Glebe House, of which at Varina, he wrote his history of Virginia. In August, 1752, he was elected President of William and Mary College, to which he removed, and over which he presided until his death in 1755.

NOTE 15. *Peter Randolph,* of Chatsworth, was the second son of the second William Randolph, of Turkey Island. He married Lucy, daughter of Robert Bolling, of Bollingbrook.

*Ms. Mem., Book of John Randolph, of Roanoke.

†Bishop Meade's Old Churches, &c, Vol. I, p. 138.

He was Clerk of the House of Burgesses, and Attorney-General of Virginia. Later, a Judge of the State Court. His portrait is at "Shirley," on James River.

NOTE 16. *Beverley Randolph*, of Turkey Island, was the first son of Wm. Randolph. He married Miss Lightfoot, of Sandy Point, and had no issue.

NOTE 17. *Major John Coles.*—Vide Note 13.

NOTE 18. *Richard Randolph, Jr.*, Member of the House of Burgesses, 1769; son of the first Richard, of Curles, married Ann, daughter of David Meade, of Nansemond County. They had issue:

I. Richard married Maria Beverly, of Blandford.

II. David Meade, b. 1769, d. September 22d, 1830; Col. of cavalry in the Revolution; m. Mary Randolph, of Tuckahoe. He was appointed Marshal of Virginia by Washington, which office he held until the Presidency of Mr. Jefferson when, being a Federal in politics, he was displaced. The Colonel and his lady were a jovial couple, and dispensed a generous and hearty hospitality. Their residence at Richmond was the commodious one now known as Allan's, (the present owner being the widow of the late John Allan, Esq., commonly termed "Jock," the patron of Edgar Allan Poe,) situated at the corner of Fifth and Main streets—the grounds of which extended to Sixth street. A frequent guest, Mr. Edmund W. Rootes, a prominent merchant of that day, of skillful rhyming capacity, of a highly facetious order, dubbed the Randolph mansion *Moldavia*, thus ingeniously uniting the christian names of host and hostess.* "*A letter from Hickory Cornhill, Esq., to his friends in the Country,*" humorously and graphically depicting in rhyme, the follies and vices of fashionable society of the beginning of the present century, when card playing, to which both sexes were addicted, was a feature of every social gathering, and the costumes were as ludicrous as they were indecent, is attributed to Mr. Rootes; claim, however, has also been

*Richmond in By-Gone Days, Second Ed., p. 127.

laid for it, for both the accomplished William Wirt, and the learned St. George Tucker, the elder. We cannot decide the question upon the intrinsic or internal character of the composition, and we are much too youthful to be able to more than transmit further the several traditions.

It was republished in the Southern Literary Messenger, May, 1838. It appears also in Mr. Mordicae's entertaining little book, "Richmond in By-Gone Days," Second Edition. He ascribes the lines to *George* Tucker.

III. Brett m. Lucy Beverley, of Blandford.

IV. Ryland m. Elizabeth Frayser.

V. Susanna m. Benjamin Harrison, Jr., of Berkeley.

VI. Jane m. Archibald Bolling, of Buckingham Co.

VII. Anne m. Brett Randolph.

VIII. Mary m. Col. Wm. Bolling, of Licking Hole, Member of House of Delegates, of Virginia.

IX. Eliza m. David Meade.

X. Sarah m. William Newburne.

NOTE 19. *William Randolph,* of Wilton, m. Anne, sister of Governor Benj. Harrison, and daughter of Benjamin Harrison, of Berkeley, and Anne, (Carter) his wife. In 1745-6 he was elected to the House of Burgesses for Goochland, vice William Randolph, of Fighting Creek, deceased.

They had issue:

I. William d. young.

II. Peter, Clerk of the House of Burgesses, in 1749. He m. first, Mary, grand-daughter of Governor Alexander Spotswood; second, Mary Page, of North River—died without issue.

III. Harrison.

IV. Benjamin.

V. Peyton m. Lucy, daughter of Gov. Benj. Harrison.

VI. Anne m. Benj. Harrison, of Brandon.

VII. Elizabeth m. Philip Grymes, of Brandon, Rappahannock County. No issue.

VIII. Lucy m. Lewis Burwell, of King's Mill. No issue.

NOTE 20. *Samuel Du Val* was a Member of the House of Burgesses in 1773; of the Virginia Convention of 1775, and an officer of the Revolution.

NOTE 21. *Rev. Miles Selden* was the son of Joseph, first settler of the name in Virginia. He was Chaplain of the Virginia Convention of 1775. A son, Miles Selden, Jr., represented the County of Henrico, in the Virginia Assembly for several years.

NOTE 22. *Thomas Adams* was one of the Delegates from Virginia to the Convention held in Philadelphia in 1778, and a signer of the articles of Confederation between the States. He was a member of the Virginia Senate of 1786, from Augusta County. He was a brother of Colonel Richard Adams, the elder.

NOTE 23. *Ryland Randolph,* son of Richard Randolph, of Curles. He inherited an ample fortune, which, remarks his sarcastic Kinsman, "of Roanoke," "he squandered to the last shilling."

NOTE 24. *Turner Southall* was a member, successively, of both branches of the Virginia Assembly for a series of years during the Revolutionary war, and afterwards. He was a zealous patriot and a highly useful citizen, being frequently elected to local offices of trust and importance.

NOTE 25. *Richard Adams.*—This was Col. Richard Adams, the elder, (son of Ebenezer, of York County,) born in 1723; died August 2d, 1800; married April 10th, 1755, Elizabeth Griffin, (sister of Judge Cyrus Griffin, of Virginia, President of the old Congress of 1788,) born 1738, died Dec. 23d, 1800. Colonel Adams was a member of the House of Burgesses 1773; of the Convention of 1775, and of the Virginia Assembly frequently afterwards. He was an enterprising and public spirited citizen, inaugurating many and fostering most of the schemes of local improvement of his day. His means were ample and his landed possessions within the limits, and in the immediate vicinity of Richmond probably more extensive than any other, then resident. His residence on Richmond or Church Hill is still standing, being the large wooden building at the corner of 22d and Grace streets, so long occupied by the late Loftin N. Ellett, Esq., and now used as a convent by the Roman Catholic Church. When first occupied by Colonel Adams it was within the outer limits of a thick grove of forest trees, a representative of which, a primeval oak, of monarchial dimensions, is still standing a few hundred yards distant, near the corner of 24th and Grace streets. Both the mansion of Col. Adams and the venerable St. John's Church were used as barracks by the British soldiery, under the traitor Arnold, during his occupancy of Richmond in 1781. The efforts of Col. Adams to induce the tide of improvement in the growing little town and embryo city of Richmond in the direction of his landed possessions on Richmond Hill, were constant and strenuous. A venerable descendant, a grand-daughter—Mrs. Eliza Griffin Carrington, now in her 83d year, relates an authentic tradition of her childhood: That quite a warm friendship at one time existed between her ancestor and Thomas Jefferson, who was a frequent guest of Col. Adams. During a visit of the former, not long preceding the Resolution of the Assembly of Virginia, to remove the seat of government from Williamsburg to Richmond, Jefferson, who was cognizant then of the measure, pledged himself to Col. Adams, in case of its success, to secure the location of the public buildings on Richmond Hill. Colonel Adams, in view of the prospective ultimate advantages in the enhancement in value of his surrounding property, promising a donation of the requisite sites, for which were proposed commanding points. The Act for the removal of the seat of government was passed June 4th, 1779,* though the definite location of the building was not indicated until the May term of 1780, when it was directed to be made upon Shockoe Hill. The following were the directors therein nominated to carry into effect the provisions of the Act, viz.: "His Excellency, Thomas Jefferson, esquire, Archibald Cary, Robert Carter Nicholas, Richard Adams, Edmund Randolph, Turner Southall, Robert Goode, James Buchanan, and Samuel Du Vall."† Mr. Jefferson incurred the life long enmity of Col. Adams because of the disappointment of the latter. Colonel Adams, at a period little later, erected, in Shockoe Creek Valley, upon the site now occupied by the depot buildings of the Chesapeake and Ohio Railroad, a substantial and spacious market house for the convenience of the residents of Richmond Hill. Three sons of Colonel Adams were also prominent and useful citizens: Colonel Richard, Jr., (born Nov. 28th, 1760, died January 9th, 1817;) Samuel Griffin, (born May 5th, 1776, died July 15th, 1821;) (both of whom served in the Virginia Assembly,) and Dr. John, (born July

*Journal Ho. of Delegates, ed. Williamsburg, 1779; p. 41.
†Hening's Statutes, X; p. 318.

14th, 1773, died June 23d, 1825,) who was, for some time, Mayor of Richmond; a daughter, Annie, (born Oct. 27th, 1762, died Oct. 27th, 1820,) married Col. Mayo Carrington, of Cumberland County. Colonel Adams and many of his descendants lie buried in the family cemetery, provided by himself, situated at the corner of 23d and Marshall streets. It occupies one-fourth of a square, and is substantially enclosed with a high brick wall. There is within our knowledge, only one other private burying-ground for the dead within the city limits, which is that of the Pickett family, immediately adjoining this, the enclosure of which has fallen to decay, and all of its tombstones have been shattered or defaced by the sacriligeous hands of wanton urchins, who, until police surveilliance was instituted, threatened to reduce the hallowed grounds of the time eloquent St. John's, to the same lamentable condition—many of its monuments presenting painful evidences of their earnest assiduity in the heartless work of mutilation and obliteration.

We are not aware that there have been any interments in the Pickett grounds for a number of years past.

Colonel Richard Adams, Jr., inherited the paternal residence; his brother Samuel erected the large mansion which formerly stood at the corner of 22d and Broad streets, and which was latterly known as Bellevue Hospital. It was destroyed by fire some years since. One of the Public School Houses now occupies its site, and Dr. John built and occupied that which is now known as the Van Lew residence, situated at the corner of 24th and Grace streets.

The descendants of Col. Richard Adams, the elder, are

still represented by family names, the most prominent and of the first social position in the State,

NOTE 26. *John Ragland* was the son of John and Anne (Beaufort) Ragland, who emigrated from Wales to the Colony of Virginia about the year 1723, and settled in Hanover Co. Grants of land to the extent of 16,000 acres are recorded in the Land Registry Office of Virginia, in the name of John Ragland.[1]

His issue was:

I. John (of the text,) married Ann Dudley, and settled in Goochland County.
II. William[2] married and had issue.
III. Samuel[2] married and settled in Louisa County. Had issue.
IV. James[2] married Catharine Davis. Had issue.
V. Evan[2] settled in Antrim Parish, Halifax Co.; married. Had issue.
VI. Pettus.[2]
VII. Martha[2] married Thomas Tinsley.
VIII. Francis[2] married Jeremiah Pate.

Pettus Ragland[2] (John[1]) married Elizabeth Davis, of Hanover County. Daughter of John Davis of Wales.

Had issue:

I. Jean,[3] born April 12th, 1755, married Wm. Chick.
II. John,[3] born July 29th, 1756.
III. William,[3] born September 17th, 1757.
IV. Sarah,[3] born February 5th, 1759, married William Rice.
V. Elizabeth,[3] born March 24th, 1760, married B. Wright.
VI. Pettus,[3] born July 8th, 1761. Moved to Halifax County.

VII. Samuel,[3] born April 12th, 1764. Died young.

VIII. Martha,[3] born Sept. 17th, 1765.

IX. Evan,[3] born Sept. 5th, 1767, married ——— Yearmans, of Louisa County. Removed to Tennessee.

X. Anne Beaufort,[3] born Oct. 7th, 1768.

XI. Nancy,[3] born July 13th, 1770, married Dr. Thomas Starke.

XII. Catharine,[3] born 1778, married John Bowe.

XIII. Fendall,[3] born 1780, died 1833, married Sarah, (died 1833) daughter of Edward and Amelia Nelson, who were cousins and descendants in the third generation of Edward, born 1690, (son of James Nelson, of Essex County, England,) who emigrated to Virginia in the year 1718, and married in 1719, Mary, the daughter of Edward and Jane Garland, of New Kent County, Va.

The issue of Fendall[3] and Sarah (Nelson) Ragland was eight sons and four daughters—of whom Elizabeth Mildred,[4] born Feb. 20th, 1814, married May 19th, 1836. Robert King, (son of John Philip and Elizabeth [King] Brock,) born December 15th, 1801, died May 27th, 1850. The editor, who is of their issue, and who has much material towards a genealogical account of the Ragland, Davis, Nelson and Garland families, would most thankfully enter into correspondence with any representative of either family who may be kindly disposed to further his object. To all such, he most heartily tenders any desired information he may have in possession.

Note 27. *John Randolph* married Francis, daughter of Richard Bland.

Issue:

I. Richard married Judith Randolph.

II. Theodrick Bland died young.

III. John, (of Roanoke) M. C. and Minister to Russia.
IV. Jane Randolph.

NOTE 28. *Nathaniel Wilkinson,* Member of the House of Delegates of Virginia, 1778-95. A prominent and most useful citizen.

NOTE 29. *Thomas Watkins.*—The Watkins family of Virginia is supposed to be of Welsh descent. The name of James Watkins appears among the early emigrants of 1608. He may have been the ancestor of the family in Virginia. The first of the name of whom anything definite is known, was Thomas Watkins, of Swift Creek, Cumberland County, whose will bears date 1760. He had eight children. His eldest son, Thomas, of Chickahominy, (of the text) is thus spoken of by the late Benjamin Watkins Leigh, his great nephew: "Of Thomas Watkins, of Chickahominy, I have heard very full accounts from my mother, (his father was the Rev. William Leigh, of Chesterfield County,) and from my uncle Thomas, both of whom knew him well. He was a man of the highest respectability, in every point of view, and in particular, a man of indefatigable industry." He reared a large family of children, four sons and seven daughters, from whom have proceeded many descendants of various family names, in Virginia and the Southern States.

His brother, Benjamin Watkins, married Miss Cary, of Warwick. He was the first clerk of Chesterfield County, which office he held until his death. He was a man of capacity and a sterling patriot. He was a member of the Convention of 1776, and took an active part in the affairs of the Revolution. One of his daughters married the Rev. Wm.

Leigh, the father of the chaste and elegant orator and able statesman, Benjamin Watkins Leigh, and the pure minded and learned Judge William Leigh, who so long and spotlessly wore the ermine. Another daughter, Francis, married Wm. Finnie, of Amelia County, from whom are descended the numerous families of Finnie, Royall, Worsham, Sydnor and others, in Virginia and North Carolina.

His son, Thomas Watkins, married Rebecca, the daughter of the Rev. Miles Selden; and one of their daughters was the first wife of Benjamin Watkins Leigh; another of Dr. Thomas Barksdale, of Halifax County.

NOTE 30. *William Randolph.*—This is presumed to be William Randolph, of Bristol, son of Isham, of Durgeness.

NOTE 31. *Boar Swamp Church.*—This church, so designated from the swamp near which it was built and which still retains its original name, was situated about twelve miles east of Richmond, upon the continuation of what is known as the Nine Mile Road. We have been informed that the original church was destroyed by fire, and another built upon its site by the Baptist denomination. The following extract determines the latter event:

"About 1773, he—Rev. Elijah Baker, began to stretch his lines, and to travel more extensively. Coming down into the lower end of Henrico, he, in conjunction with one or two others, planted Boar Swamp Church."*

The church has been frequently repaired, and its appearance, doubtless, somewhat altered. It has for a number of years past been known as Antioch Church.

*Semple's Hist. of Va. Baptists, p. 393.

NOTE 32. *Peter Winston.*—We are led to conclude this Peter Winston to have been the son of James, one of the three brothers, emigrants to Virginia.—Vide Note 13.

The issue of Peter Winston was:

I. Isaac^{2} m. Elizabeth, daughter of Capt. Wm. Burton.

II. William^{2} m. Martha Mosby, removed to Ky.

III. Peter^{2} m. Louisa Mosby.

IV. John^{2} m. Susan, daughter of Capt. John Austin, of Hanover County. Of the same family was Moses Austin, the founder of Texas, who was a merchant in Richmond in 1789. He was also engaged in the manufacture of shot, by the old method of towers, for some years. He was the contractor for covering the State Capitol with a leaden roof.

V. Susan^{3} m. Anderson Grubbs.

Isaac Winston^{2} (Peter.^{1})

Issue:

I. Emily^{3} m. Dr. Reuben Meredith.

II. Elizabeth^{3} m. Colonel Charles Parke Goodall, member of House Delegates, 1816; son of Major Parke Goodall, House of Delegates, Rev. Officer, Lieutenant of the company of volunteers of 1775, organized and commanded by Patrick Henry. Major Goodall was the proprietor of the Indian Queen Tavern, of Richmond, in "olden time." A son of Charles Parke, Charles Parke, (M. D.,) Member of House Delegates, 1864.

III. Mary^{3} m. Wm. Wingfield.

IV. Amanda^{3} m. James Williamson.

V. Thomas^{3} m. ——— Johnson.

William Winston,^{2} (Peter.^{1})

Issue:

I. A daughter[3] m. Dr. ——— Jones.

II. " m. ——— Sheppard.

Peter Winston,[2] (Peter.[1])

Issue:

Ann Crawley[3] m. John Jones.

John P. Winston,[2] (Peter.[1])

Issue:

I. Mary Ann[3] m. July 31st, 1817, Peter De Moville, of Charles City County; Member of House of Del. 1816-18. Issue—Felix[4] removed to Tennessee.

II. Peter[3] m. ——— Wood.

Issue:

Charles H., (A. M.,) Principal Baptist Female Institute, Richmond.

Susan Winston[2] (Peter[1]) m. Anderson Grubbs.

Issue:

Peter Winston Grubbs.

NOTE 33. *Mrs. Mary Randolph,* the wife of William, the first of the name who settled in Virginia. The date of her death was unknown to that indefatigable genealogist, her brilliant descendant, John Randolph, of Roanoke, and it has been obliterated by the ravages of time from her monument at Turkey Island.

APPENDIX.

A.—Bowler Cocke, p. 3, line 8. He, together with his brother, were among the patentees of the rich land of Curle's Neck, on James River, which was granted in one hundred acre lots. He was clerk of Henrico County in 1738.

B.—Four-Mile Creek, p. 5, line 13. So called from its distance from Henrico Town.

C.—James Cocke, p. 16, line 16. Clerk of Henrico County in 1699.

D.—Cornealious's, p. 22, line 38, (Cornelious's Creek.) So called from Cornelius De Hull, who owned land contiguous to it.

E.—Joseph and John Pleasants, p. 26, lines 22-3. These were the sons of John Pleasants, who emigrated to Virginia from England in the year 1665, and settled in Henrico County. The editor has in his possession a genealogical "Tree" of this family, which though unbroken as regards names, and extending almost down to the last generation, is deficient in dates. He has also manuscript material pertaining to the history of the family, who were originally, in point of religious belief, of the Society of Friends. The late Governor James Pleasants, Jr., John Hampden Pleasants, his son, the able journalist, founder and until his death in 1846 editor of the Richmond Whig, and Hugh Rose Pleasants, the brother of the latter, so well known, more recently in connection with the Richmond Press, were the descendants of Joseph Pleasants of the text. The editor desires to perfect as far as may be practicable, a genealogy of the family, and would be grateful to any of its members, who might be kindly disposed to aid him with information concerning it.

F.—Robert Pleasants, p. 70, line 2. The son of John, the younger, (vide preceding note.) He possessed a vigorous intellect, and was a man of most indomitable energy. He engaged in mercantile pursuits as well as planting, and was remarkably successful in the acquisition of wealth. He owned and resided upon the Curle's Plantation. He entered heartily into all schemes of philanthropy, and agricultural and mechanical improvements. A subject, in which he was deeply interested, was the emancipation of the African race from slavery in this country—in behalf of which he was in constant correspondence with the early advocates of the measure, both here and in England. The warmest esteem existed between him and the prominent philanthropists of Pennsylvania, Anthony Benzenet, James Pemberton, John Smith and others. Though he possessed a number of slaves, he emancipated them all by will. He conducted a correspondence with Robert Bolling, Jr., of Chellowe, Buckingham county, on the culture of the vine, the manufacture of wine in Virginia, and upon kindred subjects, in 1765-70. He died near the close of the last century.

G.—St. Peter's Church, New Kent County; vide note 11. *Rev. David Mossom.* It affords us deep gratification to be able to present the following extracts from a local announcement in the columns of the "Richmond Daily Dispatch," of the issue of November 14th, 1872, concerning this sacred relic of the past: "This old church has been substantially and beautifully repaired, and will be re-opened for service ———. The original designs which had been shamefully changed, have been restored. The high arched ceiling has been replaced, the walls replastered, finished with a hard coat, and pencilled to represent stone. A new gallery has been put up in the end of the church, and other modern improvements not inharmonious with its original design introduced. It is now one of the most beautiful, comfortable and effective of the country churches."

H.—Jonathan Boucher, page XI, second foot line. John Mercer, the editor of an abridgement of the Laws of Virginia, printed by William Parks, at Williamsburg, in 1737, in a diary kept by him in Spotsylvania county, in 1766, mentions a "Parson *Bouchier.*" Could this be adopted as the correct rendering of the name, the variable orthography of the text might readily be accounted for as apparent attempts at adaptation to its pronunciation.

I.—Page XXII, foot note. *New Church.* Since the committal of the foregoing pages to the printer, the editor has been informed that the entire walls of the New Church were erected prior to the abandonment of the work.

J.—Joseph Mayo, note 5, page 163. A recent visit of the editor to the old burying ground of the Mayo family at Powhatan,* enables him to present what he hopes will not be considered an uninteresting addition to this note.

The Cemetery is in area about fifty by one hundred feet, and is well enclosed by a brick wall—several cedar trees

---

*Now owned by Mr. Geo. S. Prince.

within the inclosure, measuring nearly two feet in diameter, are evidently of indigenous growth. The Cemetery is distant from the mansion some two hundred yards, following the current of the river, (between the two, lie the recently erected depot buildings of the Chesapeake and Ohio Railroad.) It occupies the summit of an eminence rivalling that on which is built the mansion. Its military advantages caused its selection during our late unhappy strife as the site of fortifications, which remain a little to the left of the Cemetery, almost as well-defined as when they were manned by the heroes of the "lost cause."

The Cemetery (in which there is doubtless a number of unmarked graves) contains more than a score of monuments to the dead, bearing the family names of Mayo, Poythress, Macon, Scott, Cabell, Fulton, Thom and Atkinson—among the more interesting of them are the following:

[MAYO ARMS.]

HERE lyeth interred the Body
Of JOSEPH MAYO,* Gent.,
Born in Sumersetshire,
March 25th, 1693, and died
March 25th, 1740. Aged, 47 years.
Near this Tomb, also lie Interred
The Bodys of three of his children;
who died in their infancy,
viz: JOSEPH MAYO, born March
the 28th, 1729, and died Oct. ye 9, 1732;
MARIANNA MAYO, born May ye

*The Joseph Mayo of the text.

24th, 1731, and died Sept. 5th, 1732;
STEPH., the 2d, born Sept. 18th, 1735,
and died Oct'r, 1736.

[MAYO ARMS.]
Here lyeth Interred the Body
Of GEORGE MAYO, Eldest son
of Joseph Mayo, was born
In the Island of Barbadoes,

August 30th, 1717, Died Feb. ye 19th, 1739.

The two preceding are companion stones, lying side by side, prone upon the earth. They are, in dimensions, six feet six inches in length, by three feet three inches in width, and are fully five inches in thickness, the edges being rounded into the ogee form. The material is apparently a kind of marble of great hardness and density; in color, a slatish gray. The perfect preservation of the inscriptions in all of their minutiæ and the still unmarred and polished surface of the stones, are evidences of their unusual durability. The carved inscriptions were palpably by a skilled hand. The family coat of arms being most artistically executed. The Mayo coat of arms is as follows: Azure, vair gules argent, between three coronets *or*. Crest, a unicorn's head erased, bearing a chevron vair gules and argent. Here the arms appear with a crescent for difference, and are rendered with an Esquire's helmet surmounting the shield, and an exquisite mantling of scroll work.

The two following are head-stones of gray sandstone.

Sacred
To the Memory
of

JOHN MAYO,
Who died June 17, 1786.
Aged, 50 years.
Inspired by a grateful recollection
of parental care and protection,
this stone is rais'd by Filial Affection.

Sacred
To the Memory
of,
MARY MAYO,
Spouse of J. M., who died
Sept. 1792, in the 60th
year of her Age.

Now follows a venerable couple—the tombs side by side, altar-shaped and of white marble:

In Memory of
Our Father,
WILLIAM MAYO,
Who was born in the county of Gloucester
Sept. 26th, 1757.
Died in Richmond, August 12th, 1837.
Aged, 84 years.

In Memory of
Our Mother,
ELIZABETH POYTHRESS,
Consort of William Mayo,
Born in the County of Prince George, 1759.

Died at Powhatan seat, Aug. 6th, 1806.
Aged, 47 years.

The two next are handsome monuments of white marble, obelisk in form. The inscriptions, which are presented on four sides of the one and three of the other, are as follows:

N.

Sacred
To the Memory of
Colonel JOHN MAYO,
He was born
the 21st October, 1760, at
Deep Creek, Powhatan county,
and died at
Belleville,
in the
County of Henrico,
May 28th, 1818.
Aged,
57 years and 7 months.

W.

He was endowed
with an active mind, a feeling heart,
and liberal spirit.
Richmond
will long remember his useful life,
to which she owes various
improvements,
particularly the important
Bridge
which bears his name and connects

her with
Manchester.
A work
suggested and accomplished
by individual enterprise and energy
and perseverance.
For many years
He represented Henrico
in the
General Assembly,
and was elected by that body
A Member
of the
Executive Council of State,
But earthly pageant's have passed away,
His mortal remains lies beneath this stone,
His soul humbly offers itself to God.
Reader
pray thou
with the widowed and the fatherless,
that it may be mercifully accepted
and graciously appointed to Seats of
Bliss.

N. Sacred
To the Memory of
Mrs. ABIGAIL MAYO,*
relict of the late

*Her maiden name was De Hart, and she was a native of Elizabethtown, New Jersey.

Col. John Mayo,
of Belleville,
near Richmond, Virginia,
The remembrance of her
virtues, her strength of
mind and character, her
kindness and usefulness,
will ever be cherished by
her bereft children and
friends. She lived beloved
and respected, and died
sincerely deplored,
In the the 83rd year of
Her Age.

W. Obit. 2nd of October,
Anno Domini 1843

S. Green be the turf above thee,
Mother of our other days;
None knew thee, but to love thee,
None named thee, but to praise.

E. Nat. 14th of February,
Anno Domini 1761.

We will conclude with the following inscription to the memory of two children of the late General Winfield Scott, who married a daughter of Col. John and Abigail Mayo, whose epitaphs precede this. The tomb is altar-shaped, with white marble slab and panelled slate sides, which, from the mouldering of the cement, are now falling away:

In Memory
of
Two lovely children,
JOHN MAYO SCOTT,
Born April 18th, 1819, Died Sept. 23rd, 1820,
Buried at Montpelier,
the seat of
Ex-President Madison;
And
EDWARD WINFIELD SCOTT,
Born Mar. 23rd, 1823, died May 17th, 1827,
who lies
Beneath this tomb,
Sons of
Winfield and Maria Mayo Scott.
My soul melteth away
for very heaviness,
Comfort thou me, Oh, LORD!

K.—Note 13. *Isaac Winston.* Though the origin of the Winston family in Virginia, is traditionally accepted by its members as rendered in the note, yet the following early mention of the name, which has come to the knowledge of the editor since the latter was penned, he deems it proper to offer here: He finds upon record in the Virginia Land Registry Office, grants of land to *William Winston,* the first, of date October 21st, 1687, and the last, 1706, numbering nearly 7,000 acres, and a grant of 1,079 acres in New Kent county, to *Anthony Winston,* dated October 24th, 1701.

Page 171, *lines* 11 *and* 12. The editor is now conclusively satisfied that *Isaac Winston*[1] had only two daughters, Mary and Sarah, the former of whom was grand-mother of Mrs. Madison. He extracts the following from "The Paine Family Register," No. 1, Albany, N. Y., January 1st, 1857, edited by Henry D. Paine, M. D.:

"JOHN PAYNE was an English gentleman of affluence and education. He settled in Goochland county on James river, Va. He married *Anna Fleming,* grand-daughter of Sir Thomas Fleming, second son of the Earl of Wigdon, who came to this country in 1616, and settled in New Kent county, Va., where he lived and died.

JOHN PAYNE,* his son, married Mary Coles, of Hanover county, Va.

His children were: *William, Temple, Dolly, Lucy, Anna, Mary, John and Isaac.*

WILLIAM died unmarried.

DOLLY married JAMES Madison, 4th President of the United States.

LUCY married 1st, *G. Washington;* 2d, *Hon. T. Todd,* one of the Judges of the Supreme Court of the United States.

ANNA† married Hon. *Richard Cutts,* M. C. from Maine.

MARY married Hon. *J. J. Jackson,* M. C. from Virginia.

JOHN married Miss *Wilcox,* of Canada.

ISAAC died unmarried.

L.—Page 186, line 9. Another private Cemetery has since come to the knowledge of the editor. It is located on the

*John Payne was of the religious tenets of the Society of Friends, and acted for a number of years as Clerk at their "Yearly Meetings" held in Hanover county. His penmanship, specimens of which are in the possession of the editor, was of great beauty, regularity and minuteness. It would thus appear that the marked and graceful caligraphy of Mrs. Madison was hereditary.

†"A sister of Mrs. Madison, and every way worthy of the same parentage." [*John Quincey Adams.*

north side of Lester street, between Nicholson and Louisiana streets. It contains several monuments of white marble, one of which, erected to the memory of John Prosser, who died Oct. 25th, 1810, in his 38th year, is quite handsome. It is a plinth, some four feet in height, surmounted by an urn. The only remaining name appearing, is that of Wright, and the latest inscription bears date, 1821.

St. John's Church 1741.

Interior East End St. John's Church 1774-1775,
where the Virginia Convention assembled, at which time Patrick Henry made his famous "liberty speech."

INDEX TO THE VESTRY BOOK

OF HENRICO PARISH, 1730-'73

www.ingramcontent.com/pod-product-compliance
Lightning Source LLC
Chambersburg PA
CBHW070906270326
41927CB00011B/2474

* 9 7 8 1 5 5 6 1 3 5 0 6 4 *